HOW TO EAT YO

MW01243321

Table of Contents

Chapter 1: Getting Restaurant Owners On-Board   10

Chapter 2: How to Handle Questions and Rejections   22

Chapter 3: Building Your Contact List Using Your Cell Phone   28

Chapter 4: How Do Restaurant Invasions Work as a Business?   39

Chapter 5: Extending Your Contact List Using Social Media   52

Chapter 6: How to Conduct the Restaurant Invasion   67

Chapter 7: SINALOA – Your Secret to Success   73

Chapter 8: How to Harness the Power of Yelp   80

Chapter 9: Always Hustle   84

Chapter 10: Database Collecting   91

Chapter 11: How to Use the Mass Texting App   101

Chapter 12: Emailing Your Database   104

Chapter 13: Wrapping It All Up   113

<u>Acknowledgements</u>

Thank you, F.M.

Thank you,
Tracy, Kent, White, Song, Chasing, Cyndi, An, Bae, Diec

Thank you to my love, Renee, for always pushing me to be better.

Introduction

Welcome to the world of Mobilizing People! In this book, you'll discover how to make money from eating. I'm James Hsu, the author of the book <u>Mobilizing People</u>, and the founder of an exciting, new mentorship program. Of everything I've ever done, the classes I've taught, the speeches I've given, and the books I've written, this book is what I believe to be the most important because it will open up a world of possibilities for you to make money. It teaches you step-by-step how to achieve a profitable outcome—not just theoretically, but actual, real money.

This book probably appealed to you because you were interested by the idea of getting paid to eat, and more so—getting paid a lot for it. Consider this: free meals (a no-brainer), with the added incentive of getting paid six-figures, or even half a million dollars. If it works, it's a brilliant idea, right? The good news is that it does work, and I know this because I've done it.

It's important to note that the concept of getting paid to eat will work anywhere; though you may need to tweak or change some aspects, the fundamentals and the foundations are the same wherever you live. Whether you're in Nevada like me, other parts of America, or anywhere internationally, the fundamentals work the same.

I'm excited that you're going to be a part of this experience, because this one is very special to me. So, welcome to The School of Mobilizing People. I hope you're ready to learn how to eat for free, and make up to half a million dollars doing it.

Why I Wrote This Book

Before you dive into the book, I'll tell you a little bit about myself so that we're not complete strangers. I was born and raised in Las Vegas, and I love it here because there are so many opportunities to make money!

My parents, who are Chinese immigrants, raised me with the age-old advice that I should go to school, get good grades, and get a good job. Everybody has been given similar advice. However, I wasn't strong enough academically to qualify for scholarships or admittance to any universities.

So, my parents suggested that I major in business management at the local community college so I could have a "normal" nine-to-five career. They suggested that with this degree on my resume, I'd have a better chance of getting hired. I didn't want to pursue other career choices, such as becoming a doctor or lawyer, because they required far too many years of education. So, I settled for business management because it was the fastest degree I could earn. I reasoned that with this degree, I could possibly work as a manager somewhere on the Las Vegas Strip, because all I ever really wanted was to earn a decent salary.

Throughout my teenage years, I had been a bit of a rebel. For a period of time, I sported radical-looking blonde, shoulder-length hair. I looked like an archvillain in a B movie! However, at 19 and in college, my life was abruptly turned upside down when I met my first mentor.

This gentleman was just 18 years old, and he was earning $10,000 or more each month. He was just a kid really, who didn't even attend college, and he was earning more than I imagined I could with a degree. When I say this, I'm not trying to discourage anyone from pursuing a college education—I was simply amazed that anyone could earn so much money without one! He was making $10,000 in a "bad month" and up to $20,000 when things were going good—not to mention he was younger than I was. He was making more money than my mom, who owned a motel business in Las Vegas.

In hindsight, it wasn't just the amount of money that impressed me—it was the fact that he was able to do what he wanted because he had financial freedom. I was instilled with the basic mindset of going to college, climbing the corporate ladder, and hopefully, one day I would be able to pay my own bills.

So, it wasn't just the flashy stuff that drew me in, but rather the overwhelming realization that his lifestyle and the things he was able to do—if I could achieve them—it would profoundly change my life. As a result, everything changed for me, and I'm really excited that I'm now able to pass what I've learned on to you.

When I was first introduced to my mentor, I was in a room with 100-150 people. He was on stage saying that he was open to being someone's mentor. I felt like he was talking directly to me. So, I decided right then and there: *What do I have to lose?* I'll listen to this guy, he'll teach me some things, and if it doesn't work out, at least I tried.

I started working with my first mentor when I was 19, and little did I know, it was the turning point in my life. I've since been mentored by 4 different billionaires and 15 individual entrepreneurs who are worth at least nine figures each.

Although these people make their money in different industries, the crazy thing is that the fundamentals, the basic ideas of what they taught me, were nearly identical. It truly amazed me that whether a mentor had a net worth of $100 million or $1 billion, they all had similar ideologies.

When I first met with my mentor, he asked, *"What is your skillset, and how can we harness that?"* That is the key, and that's how I got where I am today. Since then, I've published my previous book <u>Mobilizing People</u>, created an innovative mentorship program, and began my very first business venture, based on the concept that is laid out in this book: Eating for free and making half a million dollars doing it. I know it works because I've done it, so I've expanded that original idea into a step-by-step business process for you in this book.

If you already have a career, you can keep it and try these techniques part-time. If you're ready to commit full-time, you can apply the knowledge from this book and earn a real income. Overachievers, who really commit themselves, could potentially earn as much as $500,000 just by going to restaurants like I did.

It's worth noting at this point that if you're antisocial, don't like being around other people, or struggle to talk to new people, then this venture might be challenging. This endeavor requires you to be able to talk to strangers and attempt to make new friends. But, if you are willing and able, I will show you proven techniques that will help you break out of your shell.

How It All Began

For me, the concept of getting paid to eat all started in one of my favorite restaurants. It started with my very first restaurant client, Joe's New York Pizza. Joe's is where the "magic" happened, where the seed of the business concept was born.

Before we get into the fundamentals of the concept, let me explain how the idea was formulated. The idea of eating for free originally came from my mentor, who based it on the concept of Groupon. In case Groupon doesn't exist where you live, this is how it works: Any business that sells products or services can use the Groupon website to market what they sell at a cost-effective price. The business and Groupon agree on the terms of a voucher that Groupon sells to the customer. The customer then redeems the voucher for a product or service from the business, and the business and Groupon then split the profits.

So, the customer pays a discounted price for the product or service from the business on the first occasion. The business banks on the customer returning and paying full price in the future, because they were pleased with the product or service. In other words, the business is willing to take a hit on the customer's first visit using the voucher—in hopes that the lifetime value of the customer for future business will be much greater.

For example, Joe's New York Pizza places a $5 voucher on Groupon for $10's worth of pizza. A customer purchases the voucher for $5, and Joe's and Groupon split that amount. Ideally, the patron enjoys Joe's pizza enough to become a returning customer (which according to Forbes, a lifetime customer could be worth approximately $72,000).

Now that you understand how Groupon works, you can see that it benefits the customers, businesses, and of course, Groupon. With that in mind, my mentor said to me, *"James, why don't you be a walking Groupon?"* I replied, *"What do you mean?"* He explained that I should go into a restaurant, talk to whoever is in charge, and pitch the concept. So, I started pitching this idea to businesses, and not only did it change my entire perspective on business, but my entire perspective on how to make money.

Restaurant Invasions

So, with the concept of a human Groupon in mind, came the idea of Restaurant Invasions. By definition invasion means an incursion by a huge number of people into a place. So, yourself and a large group of people (that number is determined by the manager) are going to invade the restaurant. To you, this sounds like a great time out with your friends, but to a manager or restaurant owner, it means paying customers.

Imagine you and all of your friends going into a restaurant. You're taking up a lot of the real estate, everyone in that area is with your group, all this food comes out—you guys are kings! The owner and other customers will see this and it will create a buzz. The owner is making money and the customers feel like they are somewhere exciting and popular. I'll go into more detail in future chapters.

A Restaurant Invasion really can change the energy of a restaurant even during their slowest times, understanding that is critical before moving forward. Once you get that, let's get started.

Chapter 1

Getting Restaurant Owners On-Board

So by now, you're probably wondering how this concept works, and how you can eat for free and make half a million dollars doing it, right? In this chapter, I'll show you how to get started, and why this concept works. The first thing we need to do is get some restaurant owners on-board!

Getting started

The first thing you need to do is to decide on which restaurants you'd like to pitch your idea to. Once you've picked a handful of restaurants, you're ready to get started!

Before walking into any restaurant and pitching your idea, remember to dress-for-success. Do **not** walk into a restaurant dressed in shorts and a t-shirt expecting anyone to take you seriously. Make a good first impression and dress professionally. You need to make the conscious effort to dress-for-success.

Now, you're ready to walk into any food establishment and talk with the general manager, the marketing director (because this is going to be a marketing expense), or the owner (depending on the size of the business). Remember to always address people respectfully, as Mister or Miss(es) and always say, "Thank you, sir" or "Thank you, ma'am."

Although the verbiage can change, the basic ideology does not, so you approach the manager (or decision maker) by saying:

You: *Hi Mr._____, it's nice to meet you. My name is _____. Are you open to drawing more people into your business?*

I can promise you that 99% of them will reply:

Them: *Well, yeah, by doing what? What kind of marketing? How much do we have to pay you?*

You: *By paying for performance. If I don't show you results and you don't make any money from me, you don't have to pay me anything.*

Again, 99% of the time, your reply will intrigue them enough to give you a "sit-down" discussion.

Next, see whether they will talk to you right then and there. If not, you can set up an appointment. If the former, they may ask:

Them: *How long it will take?*

You: *No more than 15 minutes.*

11

Of course if you set up a meeting for the future, make sure you're there, on-time, for the appointment. When you sit down with them, you don't need a PowerPoint presentation, just the following verbal discussion.

At the appointment, you ask:

You: *When is the **slowest day** of the week and **the slowest time** of the slowest day?*

In Las Vegas, the slowest day and time was typically Tuesday at 3:00 pm, meaning that this is when the restaurant sees the least amount of business compared to any given day of the week. So, imagine they say:

Them: *Usually, Tuesdays at 3:00 pm.*

You: *How many people would you like me to bring in here this Tuesday at 3:00 pm? Would you like 5, 10, 15, 20, 30, or 40 people? I can bring 50 people into your restaurant if that's what you want. Of everything that these customers spend on their final bill, my cut will be 50% on that visit, but every time those customers return to your business for the rest of their lives, you keep 100% of the customers' spending.*

Which restaurants to approach

As you can imagine, this concept does not work for every restaurant, especially large franchises such as McDonald's, Wendy's, or KFC. In a restaurant like McDonald's, there are too many people that you would need to go through to reach the decision maker. Although some of these restaurants operate independently and can make the decision in-house, most cannot. They also don't need this kind of marketing, so focus your attention elsewhere.

Instead, try family-owned businesses, or locally-owned ones that don't have to answer to a mega-corporation or management hierarchy. These types of businesses will embrace the concept and stick with you forever.

Approaching fine dining restaurants

Fine dining restaurants have higher price points and thus, your profit will be greater.

For this type of business, you will need to introduce yourself in a more business-like manner and discuss the idea with someone of importance, at their discretion. Decide on a company name for yourself, as you need to appear professional. First, you speak to someone at the business and say:

You: *Who can I speak to about marketing your business?*

Them: *The marketing director,* or *the owner,* or *you can call this phone number.*

When addressing the marketing director or owner, you say:

You: *Hello, my name is _____. I'm the founder of XYZ. Would you like to increase your sales? Would you be open to hearing our proposition for getting more people into your restaurant?*

Them: *Well, maybe. By doing what? How much is it going to cost me?*

You: *Technically, nothing. I'm paid for performance. If I don't make you any money, you won't pay me anything. But, if I bring people in here, and you know that you're making money because of me, then you'll pay me.*

Hopefully, they'll say:

Them: *It could be interesting. How does it work?*

Schedule an appointment, or if they're ready, give them your pitch straight away, since it only takes a few minutes. The process is the same as before:

You: *When is the slowest day of the week and the slowest time of the slowest day?*

Them: *Monday at 3:30 pm.*

You: *Okay, I'll bring in as many people as you want on Monday at 3:30pm.*

Explaining the concept to the owner

Now, you introduce the idea of a 'Restaurant Invasion' to the business and explain how it benefits them.

You: *It's called a Restaurant Invasion.*

The term "Restaurant Invasion," is a good buzz word. It really seems to peak people's interest! You tell them that you'll bring in as many people as they want, whenever they want.

Although most restaurants want this done at their slowest time, others may want customers to show up at their busiest times. For example, if their busiest time was Thursday at 8:00pm, they want the "invasion" to be at 6:00pm so that people coming in at 8:00pm would see the crowd. This creates a good buzz for the restaurant as they always look busy.

Them: *What is a Restaurant Invasion? How does it work?*

You: *The way that we operate is this: if I bring in one person, and they spend $30, my share would be $15. If I set a date and I don't bring in anyone, you'll pay me nothing, and you'll lose nothing. If I bring in 1, 20, 30, 40, or 50 people to the restaurant, then whatever they spend, I get half of it. The beautiful part is that your restaurant isn't losing money, and the friends I bring in will learn how wonderful your food is. I guarantee that I'll fill up the seats and I'll get them to love the food.*

This is where you insert an example that is prevalent to the restaurant you're pitching (Mexican, Italian, etc.):

You: *You like it, I like it, everyone likes it—so that next time they're in the area, or craving pizza, they'll no longer be thinking about Pizza Hut or Dominos. Now, they'll remember how good their meal was at Joe's New York Pizza and every time they return to Joe's, you keep 100% of what they spend at your restaurant and owe me nothing.*

Also, point out that you're guaranteeing business for them by saying:

You: *Remember, I'm guaranteeing that people will come in. So whether I'm bringing in just 1 person, or 5 people, or 20 people, the restaurant is making money, right? Even if you're not making as much money the first time, my friends will remember how much they enjoyed the food here and they'll come back to Joe's New York Pizza. Isn't it true that if the food is good enough, they wouldn't care how far the drive is because they crave it?*

This script is exactly what I have used with many restaurant owners, so I know it works. I want you to read this *over and over and over and over* again so that you'll be able to recite everything verbatim. When this just rolls off your tongue and you're confident in what you're saying, I promise you that the majority of restaurant owners will say:

Them: *Okay, let's try it one time.*

Offering the benefit of social media interest

The owner or manager might want to know what other benefits the Restaurant Invasion will have, so they might ask something like:

Them: *Well, this sounds interesting. What else is going to be involved?*

You: *I'm going to make sure that all of my 'Restaurant Invasion' friends who use social media check in. All of my friends will be taking selfies together and taking photos of their food because it is so beautiful. And, I'll make sure that all of their timelines have these photos on there. Imagine that all of a sudden, 20 people are checking in on Facebook and saying that they're partying at Joe's New York Pizza.*

Social media can be another way you're marketing their business. Restaurants pay for advertisements, so you are making this worth their while. If they ask how much that will cost, you can say:

You: *Facebook advertising and social media are part of the service that we offer as a company. It's part of our 50% profit.*

Think about it like this: You bring 4 friends to Joe's New York Pizza, and they all post about it on social media. If each of you have an average of 500 friends on Facebook, this would mean, potentially, 2,000 people are seeing a free ad about Joe's. The restaurant now has free marketing from you and your friends.

Imagine that one of your Facebook friends is scrolling through their live feed and they're feeling hungry. They see that you're at Joe's New York Pizza, and they see the delicious pizza you've photographed, so they decide to go to Joe's now or on their day off.

That is the value of what you're offering, so you need to explain this to the business owners who are not social media savvy, or are not familiar with the power of word-of-mouth. These forms of advertising are so powerful that some businesses have never paid for an ad, yet have made a fortune through social media and word-of-mouth.

By becoming a restaurant invader, you will also become a professional Yelper. If you don't already have the Yelp app, download it onto your smartphone. Yelp will make you a lot of money, and I'll explain how in Chapter 9. For now, you're going to tell the restaurant owner:

You: *After I'm done eating, I'll ask the patrons that I brought to your establishment to write a review on Yelp.*

Ensure you don't say "a positive review" here, because you're not there to write fake reviews, and if they don't pay you, you're not going to be writing a positive review.

Talking contracts and payment

At this point, you need to make sure they understand that as part of the contract, they have to pay you *that day*. You need to ensure that the payment terms are stated very clearly. I always recommend that you have a lawyer review your contract.

The use of contracts may make your deals official, but it's not absolutely necessary. I say this because, if the restaurant decided that they didn't want to pay you—it wouldn't make sense, financially, to hire a lawyer to pursue a lawsuit. It would cost you far greater resources than what the deal is actually worth. Fortunately, this has never happened to me—restaurants have always paid.

Please note that at this point, you'll also want to make an agreement with the owner that you'll be eating for free. I've never had an owner push back on this request, because, remember, you are bringing them new customers that they would not have otherwise received. You are introducing a new clientele to their establishment for a small amount of money, that is generally far more expensive using other advertising vehicles. In the contract, you'll want to specify what your free meal entails including but not limited to: an appetizer, an entrée, and a drink, for example. State that this will be an addition to your financial compensation for bringing in new customers.

The final part is making sure you **confirm** with the restaurant the day before. Don't make the same mistakes I've made. I've had restaurants forget we were coming in, and as a result the restaurant was not prepared to serve an avalanche of people during a normally slow time. Fortunately, everything turned out alright, but it caused stress for the owners and myself at the time. So, remind the restaurant the day before.

The perfect pitch to business owners

Now that you have an idea of how this works, I'll give you my own 'off-the-cuff' demonstration, so that you can understand exactly how this concept works in practice. I want you to see how smooth and simple this process is.

I walk into Joe's New York Pizza, and say with a smile:

Me: *Hi, my name is James. Do you know who's in charge of marketing, or do you know if the owner is in the restaurant?*

Them: *Yes.*

Me: *Great. Do you know who that might be?*

Them: *Yes, that would be Kent Wong.*

Me: *Ok, great. Could you tell me where he is?*

Them: *Sure.*

He walks me over to Kent and I say:

Me: *Hi, Mr. Wong. My name is James. How are you?*

Kent: *Good, how are you?*

Me: *Good. Do you have a couple of minutes right now?*

Kent: *Sure.*

Me: *Great. My company, MPM, offers a service called 'Restaurant Invasions'. I wanted to see whether you'd be interested. It costs you nothing up front, and you pay for performance. Would you be possibly open to sitting down with me for 5 to 10 minutes, so I can explain exactly what I do?*

Kent: *Sure.*

Me: *Okay. Is now a good time?*

Kent: *Yes.*

Me: *Ok, great.*

I sit down with him, and say:

Me: *Basically what we do, Mr. Wong, are Restaurant Invasions. So, let me ask you this question, Mr. Wong: What is the slowest day of the week and the slowest time of the slowest day?"*

Kent: *Wednesday at 4pm.*

Me: *Ok. I could bring in 1, 5, 10, 20, 30, 40, or 50—you basically give me a number of people you're comfortable with. I can bring in as many people as you would like, and everyone pays full price. At the end of it, I get 50%, like a Groupon. Would you be open to that?*

Kent: *Yes!*

Me: *Ok, great! What time could I come in? I'd like to bring over a contract. It says pay for performance. You won't pay me unless I bring people in and they spend money at your restaurant. For everyone that I bring in, I get 50% of their final checks. And as part of my compensation, my meal is comped.*

And, that's the end of it. I'm not exaggerating. I've walked into a restaurant, met the owner for 15 minutes and we were all set. So, is it possible to set up a Restaurant Invasion after meeting the owner for only 15 minutes? Yes, because there is no risk for the restaurant. It's such an easy concept for restaurant owners to accept, especially since the owners know their own margins, and they know they're not losing money from the concept.

Of course some business owners will inevitably say no, or some will have reservations. So, in the next chapter we'll role-play some rejections you might receive.

Chapter 2

How to Handle Questions and Rejections

When it comes to being rejected, most of you are probably going to feel uncomfortable at the beginning, but don't let that deter you from trying. In this chapter, I'll show you how to overcome all the typical rejections you're likely to encounter and how to handle them. As restaurant owners dismiss your ideas with questions and rejections, you'll want to fireback with reason and logic, as to why they need to partake in your Restaurant Invasion concept.

You'll be surprised to know that you won't actually receive that many rejections. This is because restaurants know that they won't lose anything by trying the concept that you've presented. The only drawback for them is that they may not make as much profit as they intended.

You're likely to encounter questions from the restaurants, so I'll show you how to answer those too. Start by handling all questions and rejections with a smile! Then, rehearse your answers so you're not caught off-guard.

Why should I?

One question you'll often encounter is *why?* Why should the restaurant owner agree to trying out your concept?

Kent: *Why?*

Me: *Why what?*

Kent: *Why should I do this?*

Me: *It's great for businesses and I will get your restaurant more exposure. I'll bring in people who have never eaten here, who may have never thought about coming in. You and I both know the food is amazing. So, any time they're thinking "pizza", they'll no longer think Pizza Hut or Domino's. They're now going to think Joe's New York Pizza. Even if they live far from here, they'll love the pizza so much that they'll go out of their way to get to Joe's New York Pizza.*

Reply with confidence, and look them straight in the eyes.

Me: *Since my friends have had your pizza, whenever they want it again, their palates can only be satisfied with Joe's New York Pizza. So now, you have a returning customer. You're not going to be paying me when they return; you're only paying for what I'm doing now. I'm bringing in guaranteed business. Granted you may not be making as much as you traditionally would for one day, but you're creating a customer base that you did not have originally.*

What else do you offer?

Kent: *Do you do anything else?*

Me: *Yes! Every guest that uses Facebook, Instagram, or Twitter will be reminded to either 'at' (@) you or 'hashtag' (#) you if they're using social media. So, if I bring in 5, 10, 15, or 20 people—however many you're comfortable with for this first one, I'll make sure everyone checks in. Now, you'll be getting free advertising on social media that you're not even paying for. It's all part of this event. I'll make sure that they take photos of the event and take pictures of their food. It's going to be fantastic!*

When do I pay?

Kent: *When do I have to pay you?*

Me: *Because this is pay for performance, if I don't bring anyone, you don't pay me anything. If I bring 1, 50, or 100— however many we agree on, I get 50% of the total bill. After all of my friends leave, I'll wait for you to tally up the receipts and cut the check the same day.*

How often can we do this?

Kent: *How often will we do this together?*

Me: *Before we talk about any future events, which I'd love to discuss, I'd like you to try it once. I'd like you to see how simple it is and how it can increase the overall revenue for your business. That way, if you like the concept, I'd love to set up future Restaurant Invasions. But for the first one, let's see whether you're happy with the results. We'll make sure everything goes well, which I'm sure it will, and we'll go from there.*

50% is too much

Kent: *Fifty percent is too much. Can we do less?*

Me: *For this first time, we can lower it to 40%. If you're happy with the results, which I know you will be, then it would go back to 50%. But for this first one, if you feel like 50% is too much and since this is the first time we're meeting, I am definitely open to a goodwill/good faith trial. So, I'd be willing to lower it to 40% just this one time. I'll make sure in the contract that it says 40%. That way, you can experience what a Restaurant Invasion is.*

Do I need to close the restaurant to my normal customers?

Kent: *Do I need to close my restaurant to my normal customers during the invasion?*

Me: *No, your normal customers will be there too. And it's not just my group that's going to be having a great time. When we have 5, 10, 15, or 20 people in here, and all your normal customers are here, you'll notice there's more energy in the room—simply because there's more people. You'll see that even the people who aren't with my group are enjoying themselves more because of the energy of a packed restaurant. People love it when there are a lot of other people around versus going to a restaurant and it's empty.*

I can't handle that many people

Kent: *I can't handle 25 people.*

Me: *No problem. Tell me the number you're comfortable with, the time and the date you want us to set it up on, and I'll show up with that many people.*

I'm too busy

Kent: *It sounds interesting, but I'm too busy right now.*

Me: *Okay. When is a good time for me to check back in and possibly set up a date? I'd love to do our first Restaurant Invasion and show you how lucrative this can be for your business.*

Even if they don't want to do it right now, you need to leave the option open for the future. Ask them for a time in the future they might want to reconsider, and don't forget to follow up!

Are you a part of a company?

You have to remember this will be your business. So, it will benefit you to be as professional as possible.

If you can afford it, go to a CPA (Certified Public Accountant), get an LLC, and turn this officially into a **business**.

If you can't afford it, Google search something along the lines of: "How do I set up an LLC online." The benefit of doing it yourself is that it's ridiculously cheap, and you're really only paying for the cost to get your business up and running.

I'd also recommend going to your local bank and setting up a business account. Then, when owners and general managers write you a check, it's made out to your business, and not just your name.

Get business cards, so every time you go into a business you have a card with your name, and company name on it. It's little touches like this that go a long way.

When you meet the person in charge, start the conversation by giving them your business card and then say:

Hi! My name is James, I'm with MPMVSM... (revert back to the script)

So, while I doubt they will ask "Are you with a company?" It's just safer to beat them to the punch, with the line above.

Also, **never** talk in concept, for example:

It's my first time doing this and I don't know how it's going to go

Or things of that nature.

Speak in **confidence**, because the reality is, this is what you do!

Now, that you've secured the restaurant, and the owner agrees to the invasion, it is time to find your restaurant invaders. In the following chapter, I'm going to teach you how to gather a group of people to join you at the restaurant.

Chapter 3

Building Your Contact List Using Your Cell Phone

You've seen how simple it is to get a restaurant owner or manager to try the Restaurant Invasion concept. The next question you probably have is where do all of these restaurant invaders come from, and what's in it for them? In this chapter, I'll show you how to build your network of restaurant invaders.

Building a contact list

It all starts with building a list. You need to understand that you already have the people and contacts in your network to make this concept work. The first list you'll develop is your cell phone list. You'd never think that your cell phone would be one of your most valuable assets, but it's true. The "Contacts" button is going to be the most important button on your phone, and your contact list is where you're going to make all of your money. Keep in mind that we are only talking about the contacts in your cell phone for now. In Chapter 5, we will go into more details on how to build your contact list using different social media websites, as well as other networking platforms.

28

Making your list

To begin, start by texting every person you can possibly think of a few weeks prior to having your first Restaurant Invasion. You'll need to do this ahead of time to see which numbers are no longer active and which ones are still correct. Be sure to start from A-to-Z, and make note of the contacts with the incorrect numbers, as we will need to retrieve these later. At this point, you will not be inviting your list to the Restaurant Invasion just yet. You're simply checking which numbers are still active and catching up with people you haven't spoken to in a while.

It's important to note that you shouldn't invite a contact to show up to a Restaurant Invasion out of the blue if you haven't talked to them in a while. In most cases, if you invite someone you haven't spoken to recently, they probably won't show up. This means you need to speak with the person regularly before extending an invitation to them. Part of this business involves regularly communicating with people you hope to invite to your Restaurant Invasions.

It's helpful to make a list of people you might be interested in inviting to the Restaurant Invasion, then reach out to them with some sort of communication— preferably a phone call, but text is fine too—**twice a week at a minimum**. That way, your invitation won't seem to come out of left field when you do extend the invitation.

The first text – just over two weeks before the event

So, for the first message, you'll need to text each person you're inviting **at least two weeks before** the planned event. The text has to sound natural. The goal here, is to make small talk, and eventually invite them out for food. Don't make it sound business-related, just be personable. For example, if the first person in your contact list is called Angela, text her and say, *"Hi, Angela. How've you been?"*

Continue down your list of names with the same text, *"Hi, _____. How've you been?"*

You might be texting people for hours, but this is just a part of running your business. Just remember that these texts are getting you closer to that six-figure income.

Eventually, I recommend using a mass texting app to invite people, which we will cover in Chapter 11. But for now you'll need to create your list organically, first by personalizing each text. At the beginning, it's important that you do **not** mass text these people. They need to know that this isn't business-related—just personal.

So when you first text Angela, just say:

You: *Hi, Angela. How've you been?*

Them: *Great! How are you?*

Keep it friendly, and do not mention Restaurant Invasions:

You: *How's the family? What have you been up to?*

This conversation is all about chatting and catching up. Ask broad, open-ended questions that invite conversation, rather than closed-ended questions that can be answered with "yes" or "no". Again, don't mention the Restaurant Invasion during this conversation.

The invitation – two weeks before the event

Then, 48 to 72 hours later, you text her again:

You: *Hey, Angela. What's up?*

When she texts back, keep the banter light and friendly:

Them: *Pretty good. It's my day off.*

You: *Great!*

This is when you strike with the restaurant invitation. If you've set the date for Joe's New York Pizza on Wednesday at 4:00 pm in two weeks' time, say:

You: *Me and a bunch of friends are eating at Joe's New York Pizza the Wednesday after next at 4pm. I don't know if you've been there before, but I wanted you to come! You can bring your girlfriend/boyfriend/best friends/a couple of friends. You can come, yes?*

Ending the conversation with something like *"You can come, right?"* is called an **assumptive close**. This elicits a direct answer, either *"yes"* or *"no"*.

In the United States, this is an appropriate conversation, but in some countries or cultures, this might come across as being rude or too straight forward. In that case, you may need to modify this text depending on your location and culture, or the culture/country of the person you are speaking to.

At this point, they might reply with something like:

Them: *I wish I could, but I'm only available in the mornings before 10 am,* or *weekends are better for me.*

So now, with this information, you're going to fill out your contact's days-off schedule.

Days-off schedule

As you start to invite your contacts, you'll notice that people will say things like "I would **but** I'm only off Tuesday or Wednesdays." Bank tellers for instance, are off on Sundays. In Las Vegas, casinos are open 24/7 so casino employees have unpredictable days off. These days, not everyone works a 5-day, 9-5 or 9-6 traditional work week.

You need to remember when your friends are off, so use a Microsoft Word or Excel document, or an iPad to keep a calendar of this information. List the days of the week, and enter your contacts' names under the days when they're typically off. For example, your days-off schedule might look like this:

MON.	TUES.	WED.	THURS.	FRI.	SAT.	SUN.
Jane	Helen	Joyce	Susie	Brian	Violet	Cindy
Kent	Kent	Tracy	Phyllis	Scott	Theo	Theo
Ashley	Aaron	Aaron	Mike	Mike	Ruby	Jake

This will make your work much easier and more efficient. Now, for future invasions you won't waste time texting people who won't be available that day. Thus, you can spend your time communicating with those who will be off and can potentially come to the invasion.

While not everyone will be off on the day you've planned a Restaurant Invasion, at least a few people will be at the start. Get your friends scheduled in before they schedule something else. When you invite people with a few weeks' notice, most people don't have anything planned for their days off, so the beauty of this is that you're giving people something to look forward to on their days off.

You'll start to notice that if you create an environment that people love—events that are fun and exciting—then if people are off on the day you've scheduled the event, they *will* come. Once someone likes you, they'll always go to any event you offer if they're off. Whether you have a Restaurant Invasion once a day, once a week, or once a month, if they're available, they'll be there. Once people start going, they'll keep going because they love it!

This list also comes in handy when scheduling future events. For instance, you may discover that a lot of people have Tuesdays off. So you might try to schedule an event for Tuesday lunchtime or Monday evening. Eventually, you'll build a list where you have 50 names on Monday, 50 names on Tuesday, 50 names on Wednesday, and so on. Then if your restaurant owner wants an event on a Wednesday, you'll go to your Wednesday list and start inviting people.

The confirmation text – one week before the event

So, you've chatted with your contact, you've invited them, and they've said they can make it (and so on through your contacts list). You now have a head count of who can make the Restaurant Invasion. Once you've obtained all of your attendees, text them a week ahead to confirm:

"Hey Angela, I'm so excited to see you next Wednesday at Joe's New York Pizza [Give them the address here]! It's been a while, plus we get to eat great food. Our reservation is at 7pm, so if you can arrive around 6:45pm, that would be beautiful. Just a heads up, I'm pumped for you to see my new little gig, going to businesses, rating them, doing some promoting to make some extra income, plus I now get to see you and hang out for a few. Also I wanted to confirm, were you going to bring anyone?"

Always end the text with a question where they have to respond. I like "Were you going to bring anyone?" because they might have forgot to invite their best friend or partner. This reminds them and hopefully will now add another person to your list. To get a headcount, ask:

You: *How many people will you be bringing so that I can make sure there's a large enough table for us?*

Angela: *Yes, I'm going to be there, and I'm bringing both my boyfriend and my roommate.*

Now, if you're using Excel, separate your contact list into columns, so you can manage it better. Since Angela has confirmed she's bringing 2 people, on the list under her name, write 2. If they don't plan to bring guests, just list their name. For example:

ANGELA	FREDERICK	ASHLEY	JOHN	HILARY	ROMAN	BOB
2		1	3	5	2	

You can also easily use your iPhones Notes application for this, for example:

Joe's New York Pizza
Wednesday April 11, 2018 (current Headcount)

Ashley	4
Chasing	2
Tracy	3
Cindy	2
Aaron	1
Song	2
Preston	1
DMW	1
Bryan	5
Angelica S.	3
Sharon L.	1
Jessica P.	4
Hope	2
Dj Duran	2
Elmer	2
Dallas I.	3
Craig	2
Latasha	5
Chris H.	1
Jill	2
Tina	2
Joy	4
Taylor B.	3
Brenda	1
Serena	3
Issac P.	2
Adam J.	1
Don W.	2
Jordan F.	5
Dallas R.	2
Jenny	3
Tod L.	1
Jeremy	4
Nathan D.	3

The wonderful thing about these lists is that when you have future events, you can go back to every old event list and re-invite those people to new restaurants.

Getting your contacts to bring other guests

The idea here is to get your contacts to bring other people, so you can **grow your business** by gaining new contacts. When I first started this concept, I asked one of my personal friends to bring a couple of people. She ended up bringing 5 people with her. In a Restaurant Invasion, the more people the better.

If the restaurant owner wanted at least 20 people, it's best to always over deliver rather than underdeliver—get a head count of 30 people instead. If you show up with 10 people when you promised 20, it will look bad. But, if you promised 20 and show up with 25-30, it proves to the restaurant owner that you are serious, and there are 30 people who are ready to eat. Most restaurants you are approaching seat at least 50 guests, and have sufficient food on hand to serve plenty of people. So if you've promised 20 and bring 25 or 30, it's not an imposition for the restaurant—they'll actually be happy to have the customers.

The added benefit is that if you haven't seen your contact for a while, inviting them to bring their friends or partner will make them feel more comfortable, because they'll be with someone they speak to regularly. You'll be surprised by how many people you don't see that often who actually find it nice to meet up, eat, and catch up if they can bring someone they know well. Don't forget, people like to be invited and have opportunities to go out!

The reminder text – the day before the event

The day before the event, remind everyone who is coming. Text the person first, and if they don't respond within 5 hours, give them a direct call (sometimes they're at work, so give them time to respond on a break or to get off work). It's smart to do the confirmation text in the morning, because if you text someone at 3pm and they don't respond by 8pm, it's too late to call them.

Give them the address again in case they've lost it. Then when they reply to confirm, say "See you tomorrow. Excited to see you!"

Meeting new contacts

If you meet someone completely new, for example while grabbing a coffee at Starbucks, you'll follow the same process. Send them a text saying it was nice to meet them. Don't pitch them at first. Take an interest in their life and engage in small talk. Take notes about what they care about and record it under the notes section of their contact information.

You: *Hey nice to meet you.*

Make small talk, send them your Facebook details, and connect. Two days later, you can then invite them to your Invasion:

You: *Hey, not sure if you're free. I host Restaurant Invasions. I'd love for you to attend and introduce you to all my friends who are coming, it's super fun. Can you come?*

Then follow the same process. Simple, right?

In the next chapter, I'll show you why and how this works as a business.

Chapter 4

How Do Restaurant Invasions Work as a Business?

Now that we've covered the early stages of the Restaurant Invasion, such as pitching managers and creating a contact list, it's time to look at what you are doing as an actual business.

Why would restaurant owners agree to this?

You may be wondering why any business would agree to this, since they're giving away a cut of their profit. There are a couple things to note about the restaurant business that answer this question. The first is that businesses have huge profit margins on their food. They might potentially have huge profit margins for other aspects of business as well (such as beverage, retail, etc.), depending upon how efficiently the business operates.

For instance, if you're paying $7 or $8 for a slice of pizza, and it costs the business only 50 cents to $1 to make that slice of pizza, the restaurant owner then profits $6 to $7 per slice. In your case, the value of that same slice of pizza is worth $3.50 - $4 since you're negotiating with the business owners to take half of the bill. So, even if you take half of their sale, you know that the business is not losing any money, as they're still making $3 to $4 in profit on every slice.

The next vital thing to keep in mind is that restaurants do **not** make money unless orders are going through. If there are 50 marinated steaks in the refrigerator with no one eating it, or a cooler full of sodas that no one is drinking, then the business is losing money if the food spoils and goes to waste.

Additionally, you'll be giving businesses free advertising by getting your restaurant invaders to check in online and leave reviews. This increases the business' social media presence without additional cost. This is ideal for small businesses, and independent or family-run restaurants, since they may or may not have the budget for additional advertising. And, since you're offering free advertising, they don't pay anything upfront unless you're bringing people to the restaurant to eat. Understand that **you** are adding value to their restaurant, and you can have confidence in that when you pitch the idea to the business.

Why would your contacts agree to this?

It's easy to see why restaurant owners would agree, but why would your contacts be interested? Why would they take part?

The first reason that people agree to this is because of **you**—the person who invited them. They like you, so they want to see you and catch up. Even if they haven't seen you in a while, they'll feel comfortable because you've told them they can bring a friend or partner. Wouldn't you feel more comfortable catching up with someone you haven't seen in ages if you could bring your partner or best friend?

Secondly, you'll be surprised to know that, most of the time, people don't really have anything to do on their days off. Especially if you're inviting them to something a few weeks in advance and they have nothing planned. They're going to eat somewhere anyway, and if they're going out, then why not with you? If they were going to be cooking at home, then you're offering them a more exciting opportunity. You're actually giving people something to look forward to on their days off.

It's important to realize you're adding value. You are putting together an opportunity for people to socialize. Humans are social creatures who *want* to socialize. In my experience, the majority of people want to go out, but need an excuse to do it. So when you're inviting someone who enjoys your company, they'll probably come along if they're free. You'll discover that if you put events together, people *will* attend them.

You may be reading this thinking to yourself, "Asking people to attend my event may anger, or annoy, them." In fact, the opposite is often true. Who doesn't want to be invited to a birthday party—even if they RSVP with regrets, they're happy to be invited and hurt if they weren't invited. The simple fact is, most people enjoy going out, having new experiences, and meeting new people.

Often, people go to the same places, with the same friends, to the same restaurants, and do the same activities. They go out to eat with the same two or three people every time. Usually, they are buried in their smartphones and the conversations are the same ones, because they literally text, talk, and interact with these same people every day.

Thus, people are bored with "the same." They want new experiences. So, when you offer them a new environment with some new people and new conversations, but let them bring people who they are comfortable with, it works. If they're invited out somewhere new, in a non-threatening way (remember, you're not selling them a timeshare or a multi-level marketing scheme, just a fun night out), then you're enriching their lives. People will be pleased to be included, to be invited, to have a chance to break from their otherwise dull routine.

Even in Las Vegas, the home to hundreds of nightclubs and entertaining shows, people get bored with routine and want to do something exciting off of The Strip.

They want to get together, have dinner with their friends, and do something different. This concept is unique because it offers your friends and contacts something completely out of the norm.

Why is this going to work for you?

This is where the magic of eating for free and making six-figures comes into play... All you're really doing is *inviting people to come out and eat with you*. So there's something about event planning and Restaurant Invasions that isn't really "work." Of course it is *technically*, but it's also just friends hanging out and enjoying food together.

The simple truth about this whole concept is that you can sit comfortably on your couch, text people, and introduce them to new restaurants. In most cities, there are an endless number of restaurants to eat at, so there will always be somewhere new to try.

Another reason this works is because you'll likely be the only other person that's doing it where you live. This concept is unique. And, even though the United States has over 300 million people, the likelihood of anyone else doing this in your particular market is slim to none.

How does this work as a business?

It works because it's simple. What we have here is a business opportunity that doesn't involve a ton of equipment, college degree, or even a startup loan. All it requires is a handful of friends, a social media account, a phone—and you most likely already have those things.

You can eat for free and make half a million dollars by simply taking advantage of any social media account (which you probably already use), your cell phone (which you probably already have), and building relationships with people (who you already know). You already have some friends, which means you have access to your friend's friends too using social media. Your job is to harness this knowledge and make money from it.

So, is this a business? **Yes.**

Can you make a six-figure income if you do everything I'm telling you to do and you do it correctly? **Yes.**

Is this a serious enough business that will make you a lot of money? **Yes**.

In order to make a six-figure income, you're going to need to expand your business. As you start doing this, you'll also find people saying to you, *"This is cool. I want to get in on it, too."* If you get 50%, you can offer them 50% of what you're getting, or whatever amount you agree to (that's entirely up to you). This way, you can develop the business simply by bringing others on board.

For now, you need to factor in the potential earnings, so use a simple Excel document, for example:

Potential Earnings Table

Days in a Week	# of Customers	Average Meal Price	Your Take-Home Pay	1 Meal/5 Days/Week	$6,500
1	5	$10	$25	1 Meal/7 Days/Week	$9,100
2	5	$10	$50	2 Meal/5 Days/Week	$13,000
3	5	$10	$75	2 Meals/7 Days/Week	$18,200
4	5	$10	$100	3 Meals/5 Days/Week	$19,500
5	5	$10	$125	3 Meals/7 Days/Week	$27,300
6	5	$10	$150	4 Meals/5 Days/Week	$26,000
7	5	$10	$175	4 Meals/7 Days/Week	$36,400

Days in a Week	# of Customers	Average Meal Price	Your Take-Home Pay		
				1 Meal/5 Days/Week	$13,000
1	5	$20	$50	1 Meal/7 Days/Week	$18,200
2	5	$20	$100	2 Meal/5 Days/Week	$26,000
3	5	$20	$150	2 Meals/7 Days/Week	$36,400
4	5	$20	$200	3 Meals/5 Days/Week	$39,000
5	5	$20	$250	3 Meals/7 Days/Week	$54,600
6	5	$20	$300	4 Meals/5 Days/Week	$52,000
7	5	$20	$350	4 Meals/7 Days/Week	$72,800

Days in a Week	# of Customers	Average Meal Price	Your Take-Home Pay		
				1 Meal/5 Days/Week	$19,500
1	5	$30	$75	1 Meal/7 Days/Week	$27,300
2	5	$30	$150	2 Meal/5 Days/Week	$39,000
3	5	$30	$225	2 Meals/7 Days/Week	$54,600
4	5	$30	$300	3 Meals/5 Days/Week	$58,500
5	5	$30	$375	3 Meals/7 Days/Week	$81,900
6	5	$30	$450	4 Meals/5 Days/Week	$78,000
7	5	$30	$525	4 Meals/7 Days/Week	$109,200

Days in a Week	# of Customers	Average Meal Price	Your Take-Home Pay		
1	5	$50	$125	1 Meal/5 Days/Week	$32,500
2	5	$50	$250	1 Meal/7 Days/Week	$45,500
3	5	$50	$375	2 Meal/5 Days/Week	$65,000
4	5	$50	$500	2 Meals/7 Days/Week	$91,000
5	5	$50	$625	3 Meals/5 Days/Week	$97,500
6	5	$50	$750	3 Meals/7 Days/Week	$136,500
7	5	$50	$875	4 Meals/5 Days/Week	$130,000

Days in a Week	# of Customers	Average Meal Price	Your Take-Home Pay		
1	10	$10	$50		
2	10	$10	$100		
3	10	$10	$150		
4	10	$10	$200	1 Meal/7 Days/Week/Year	$18,200
5	10	$10	$250	2 Meals/7 Days/ Week/Year	$36,400
6	10	$10	$300	3 Meals/7 Days/Week/Year	$54,600
7	10	$10	$350	4 Meals/7 Days/Week/Year	$72,800

Days in a Week	# of Customers	Average Meal Price	Your Take-Home Pay		
1	10	$20	$100		
2	10	$20	$200		
3	10	$20	$300		
4	10	$20	$400	1 Meal/7 Days/Week/Year	$36,400
5	10	$20	$500	2 Meals/7 Days/Week/Year	$72,800
6	10	$20	$600	3 Meals/7 Days/Week/Year	$109,200
7	10	$20	$700	4 Meals/7 Days/Week/Year	$145,600

Days in a Week	# of Customers	Average Meal Price	Your Take-Home Pay		
1	10	$30	$150		
2	10	$30	$300		
3	10	$30	$450		
4	10	$30	$600	1 Meal/7 Days/Week/Year	$54,600
5	10	$30	$750	2 Meals/7 Days/Week/Year	$109,200
6	10	$30	$900	3 Meals/7 Days/Week/Year	$163,800
7	10	$30	$1,050	4 Meals/7 Days/Week/Year	$218,400

Days in a Week	# of Customers	Average Meal Price	Your Take-Home Pay		
1	10	$50	$250		
2	10	$50	$500		
3	10	$50	$750		
4	10	$50	$1,000	1 Meal/7 Days/Week/Year	$91,000
5	10	$50	$1,250	2 Meals/7 Days/Week/Year	$182,000
6	10	$50	$1,500	3 Meals/7 Days/Week/Year	$273,000
7	10	$50	$1,750	4 Meals/7 Days/Week/Year	$364,000

Days in a Week	# of Customers	Average Meal Price	Your Take-Home Pay		
1	15	$10	$75		
2	15	$10	$150		
3	15	$10	$225		
4	15	$10	$300	1 Meal/7 Days/Week/Year	$27,300
5	15	$10	$375	2 Meals/7 Days/Week/Year	$54,600
6	15	$10	$450	3 Meals/7 Days/Week/Year	$81,900
7	15	$10	$525	4 Meals/7 Days/Week/Year	$109,200

Days in a Week	# of Customers	Average Meal Price	Your Take-Home Pay		
1	15	$20	$150		
2	15	$20	$300		
3	15	$20	$450		
4	15	$20	$600	1 Meal/7 Days/Week/Year	$54,600
5	15	$20	$750	2 Meals/7 Days/Week/Year	$109,200
6	15	$20	$900	3 Meals/7 Days/Week/Year	$163,800
7	15	$20	$1,050	4 Meals/7 Days/Week/Year	$218,400

Days in a Week	# of Customers	Average Meal Price	Your Take-Home Pay		
1	15	$30	$225		
2	15	$30	$450		
3	15	$30	$675		
4	15	$30	$900	1 Meal/7 Days/Week/Year	$81,900
5	15	$30	$1,125	2 Meals/7 Days/Week/Year	$163,800
6	15	$30	$1,350	3 Meals/7 Days/Week/Year	$245,700
7	15	$30	$1,575	4 Meals/7 Days/Week/Year	$327,600

Days in a Week	# of Customers	Average Meal Price	Your Take-Home Pay		
1	15	$50	$375		
2	15	$50	$750		
3	15	$50	$1,125		
4	15	$50	$1,500	1 Meal/7 Days/Week/Year	$136,500
5	15	$50	$1,875	2 Meals/7 Days/ Week/Year	$273,000
6	15	$50	$2,250	3 Meals/7 Days/Week/Year	$409,500
7	15	$50	$2,625	4 Meals/7 Days/Week/Year	$546,000

Once you start locking in your invasions, you'll be able to calculate how much money you're expected to make by determining the number of customers you're going to have at each restaurant, the average bill (per person), the percentage you made with the owner, and so on.

You can also use your Notes app to keep track of this, for example:

```
Joe's New York Pizza
Wednesday April 11, 2018 (current Headcount)

Ashley        4
Chasing       2
Tracy         3
Cindy         2
Aaron         1
Song          2
Preston       1
DMW           1
Bryan         5
Angelica S.   3
Sharon L.     1
Jessica P.    4
Hope          2
Dj Duran      2
Elmer         2
Dallas I.     3
Craig         2
Latasha       5
Chris H.      1
Jill          2
Tina          2
Joy           4
Taylor B.     3
Brenda        1
Serena        3
Issac P.      2
Adam J.       1
Don W.        2
Jordan F.     5
Dallas R.     2
Jenny         3
Tod L.        1
Jeremy        4
Nathan D.     3

84 People come to the invasion

Total Receipts:
$2,877

Average Check: $34.25

Your cut: $1,438.50
```

Now that you understand how and why this works, we'll move on to a bigger network that will help you grow your business and earn more money—social media.

Chapter 5

Extending Your Contact List Using Social Media

Although your cell phone list is useful, it is very limited. Luckily, we live in a time where your resources are endless, thanks to social media. Because of Facebook and other social media applications, your life is much easier as your contact list is everywhere. I'm pretty confident that most people nowadays have a Facebook account, which is a perfect networking platform. If you don't have a Facebook account, please sign up for one immediately.

A network is why people like Mark Zuckerberg of Facebook, or Evan Spiegel, Bobby Murphy, and Reggie Brown Poster, the owners of Snapchat, have such valuable sites. It's not solely because Facebook or Snapchat are great ideas, which they are, but because they have extensive databases of first and last names, email addresses, phone numbers, and different ways to connect with their target markets. You are going to become a human mobilizer, and your contact list is your way to succeed.

One of the most important lists you have is your friends list on Facebook. Almost everybody has a Facebook account, but if you live in a country where another form of social media is predominant, you can use that instead. In this chapter, I'll base most of my examples on Facebook, but the idea is transferable to any form of social media you use.

Filling in the gaps in your cell phone list

In Chapter 3, you used your cell phone and started by texting everyone in your contact list. You might have found that some of the numbers either no longer work, or someone you didn't know responded instead. So, for anyone whose number was incorrect, find them on Facebook and send them a personal message.

Never write on people's Facebook wall or timeline. It's considered bad social media etiquette, and people hate having things written on their timeline without them being able to approve it first. Some people also don't want their social media network knowing if they've attended Restaurant Invasions, so leave it up to people whether they choose to advertise this.

The direct message will say the following:

You: *Hey, I sent you a text, but it went to some random person. I think I wrote down the wrong number when I saved it to my phone. Would you mind sending it to me again or texting me on XXX-XXX-XXXX. It'd be great to keep in contact.*

When they text you, save their number and contact information in your phone.

My contact list was short when I started, so don't worry if yours is too. If I could go back in time and tell my teenage-self to save every number in my cell phone and keep in contact with all my friends, I would. Never underestimate the power of a database—it made Mark Zuckerberg a billionaire! As you can see, an incredible database is an immeasurable tool.

Extending your list further

After you've gathered the updated information for your cell phone contacts from Facebook, you can begin working your way through your friends list on Facebook for the numbers that you don't have in your phone. You may have hundreds—or even thousands—of Facebook friends, and although it may seem tedious, this is an important part of the process.

Again, when you're contacting those on your friends list, do **not** write on their timeline and remember to make it **personal**. So, go through your friends list on Facebook and compare it with your cell phone until you find the first person without a contact number. Imagine the first person without a number is named Kent. Then send Kent the following direct message:

You: *Hey, what's up my friend! Haven't seen you in a long time. Was going through my phone and just realized I don't have your number. Me and a bunch of friends are going out for dinner, and wanted to see if you'd be interested in coming. Text me back so you won't forget,* or *reply back with your cell phone number, and I'll text you.*

Do not copy-and-paste your message, as people will think it's spam. Rewrite my previous message and add your personal touches to ensure it sounds like you. Otherwise, they probably will think your account was hacked, and won't respond. You can't cut corners and expect to make half a million dollars. Direct message your friends and be sure to make your messages personal.

This is how you start expanding your cell phone list. You can have over 10,000 real cell phone numbers just by finding your friends through Facebook and direct messaging everyone. Every time you get a new number, transfer that information into your cell phone, and then start texting every single person listed in your phone to invite them to eat with you. Simple, right?

Finding more friends

Once you've gained the numbers of everyone on your own friends list, move on to your wider network—your "mutual friends" and "suggested friends." On Facebook, you'll find that your friends have friends that you actually know. Perhaps you're not Facebook friends with this person yet because you don't know them well, or maybe you went to high school at the same time as them, but don't know them personally.

Some people might find it strange if you connect with them, but most will realize you're a friend of a friend, or someone they went to high school with, and accept the request. Then, it is your job to mobilize, or become friendly, with them.

Your goal now is to gain 10 new friends a day through this wider network. If you add 10 new friends a day, then in 30 days, you'll have 300 new friends, and potentially 300 new numbers. And, with those 300 new numbers comes potentially 600 new numbers if each of those 300 numbers bring just 1 person to your event.

F.O.R.M.

Now, maybe you are starting to panic at the idea of talking with strangers or adding mutual friends you may not know. Well, part of making this successful is being able to connect with people, even individuals you don't know. If you have stage fright, or social anxiety, that might be your biggest challenge going forward. That's why I always advise people to get out of their comfort zone. The more you put yourself in situations you aren't comfortable with, the more comfortable you become.

Before I get to F.O.R.M., if you don't want to immediately create a conversation with a new "mutual friend," just subtly show friendly gestures. Once they've added you, write them a message and say, "*Thank you for the add (Name).*"

You've opened the door to a later dialogue, but you don't have to immediately walk through it. But, at least it's open.

From this point on, **every time** you see them post something, be sure to LIKE their post. Show you are supporting their content. Even, throw in a nice comment or two. People like seeing others liking and supporting their posts or content.

After a good week or two of liking their posts, private message them and start that dialogue.

Now, when it comes to actually talking with strangers via Facebook or in person, remember: F.O.R.M.

F - Family
O - Occupation
R - Recreation
M - Money

Start with generic openings:

Hi! How are you?

How's your day going?

Then, start implementing F.O.R.M.:

How long have you been in Las Vegas?

*Did you move here with your **family**?*

What do you do for work? or *What's your **occupation**?*

What do you like to do for fun? (Recreation)

When it comes to money, obviously never outright ask someone "Do you have money?" You go over this question by understanding what they do for fun and what they do for work. This part (of F.O.R.M.) gives you an idea what they spend their money on, and if food or art, for example, is something that is important to them.

Start these conversations with people and your goal is to get them to talk 90% of the time, and you speak 10% of the time.

God, the universe, or whatever deity you may believe in, gave us two ears and one mouth for a reason. **Shut up** and **listen** to others. People really enjoy talking about themselves, even if they don't admit it, and people like other individuals who listen to them.

So, once you've finished with F.O.R.M., you should have plenty of branches to reach for (food, their job, their family). Then, just start having a regular conversation.

Practice this until you have perfected it, and it just becomes a part of you.

If you never want to have a strange conversation with someone ever again, you need to F.O.R.M. them.

If you want to be able to hold a conversation with anyone, at any age, you must master F.O.R.M.

Then, once you are friendly and things feel comfortable, you can invite them to a Restaurant Invasion.

Remember, since you don't know each other that well, these 300 new friends will probably want to bring their significant other, or best friend, to dinner with you. You'll tell them that you're bringing friends and tell them to bring a bunch of their friends, so they'll most likely bring at least one new person. That's 600 new friends, or more, since each new person has an entirely new circle of friends that you don't know.

Do you realize that if you do this for 6 months, you could have 3,600 new numbers? And that figure doesn't include friends who bring friends, who bring friends, who bring friends, who bring friends, and so on.

Other social media

Although Facebook is a major component to building your network of restaurant invaders, it is not the only answer, and it's not the only type of social media that can help. I haven't discussed Instagram or Twitter, but the principles are exactly the same. If you're not big on Facebook, but you have a network on Twitter, then befriend your friends' friends on Twitter, direct message them, and ask them for their phone numbers.

However, if you don't have Facebook, I strongly encourage you to join the site. The statistics say that 3.5 billion people have internet access, and 1 billion of those have Facebook. Furthermore, founder Mark Zuckerberg wants to offer free internet access to everybody, so the network is set to grow. As you can see, Facebook gives you access to an endless supply of contacts which can translate to a huge income.

What if I don't know anyone on any social media platforms?

I know what some of you may be thinking: "I don't know anyone. I mean, I know some people, but not enough to fill a Restaurant Invasion. What do I do?" This is the most common worry I hear expressed by people who consider pursuing this business.

Don't worry. You're not alone. I know that I have a large network and, for me, getting a big group together for an invasion is relatively easy. I also know that many of you reading this book probably haven't been involved in any type of networking like I have, and you probably don't have access to a lot of people that you can invite to a Restaurant Invasion.

So what do you do if you don't know a lot of people? You go to social situations, events, where a lot of other people who like to network go. You go to places where people who, by virtue of the fact that they are in a particular setting have demonstrated that they want to connect with others, are. What are people who like joining groups doing with their free time? Joining groups, obviously.

Fortunately, there's a website for people who like to join groups and meet new people. In fact there are a few, but there's one primary website: MeetUp.com.

To be clear, I am not proposing that you set up your own MeetUp group. Although, you can do this at some point in the future. Knowing that many of my readers would struggle with this part of the business—meeting and inviting large numbers of people to events—I took it upon myself to learn how to master MeetUp.com.

Initially, I tried setting up my own MeetUp group on the website. Hardly anyone joined my group. #fail. I even had a detailed write-up for my MeetUp group that made the Restaurant Invasion sound super cool and exciting. Nobody signed up. In hindsight, I'm not surprised. This is a new concept. Nobody goes to Google and searches for "Restaurant Invasion." Even when I changed my description and named it a "networking event" nobody signed up. Why? Branding. Nobody knew who I was, I used a fake name so that I couldn't win just by being James Hsu (who a lot of people in Las Vegas know). That wouldn't teach me how to make this successful for my readers. I created a generic name for my postings—the

Asian equivalent of John Smith. I was Mike Lee. As Mike Lee, without a picture, I was just some random nobody posting a MeetUp group. Why would anyone join it? If I was offering $100 bills I can only assume that a few people would join, but otherwise it's doubtful. It's scary. People don't generally take risks with their time. So, as an unknown, setting up a new MeetUp.com group, you probably won't get any sign-ups.

So what did I do? I attended other people's large and well-attended MeetUp events. Well, technically, I didn't attend. I had my students sign up and attend. These students are not like me. They don't go to these events with my people skills. They are not business owners or super-human networkers by any standard. They were just guys in their 20s and 30s, working this business the way you will be.

So how did it turn out for them? First, let me tell you that each of these three students of mine attended one MeetUp event, every day for seven days. That's a lot of MeetUp events in a week. Each of them participated in the various MeetUp events that they had signed up for: networking events, mini-golf, whatever they were. Each one worked to meet people, and ask people they met for their contact information, either their Facebook name, their phone number, or their Instagram, whatever was that person's go-to social media.

The beauty of Facebook is that virtually everyone has one and it's not "strange" or "weird" to literally just take out your phone, click on Facebook, leave it on the search bar and, without a word, someone would know exactly what you want them to do. Obviously, don't do it like that but your job, no matter what type of MeetUp you go to, is to make friends, and before you leave them, pull out your phone and ask them to connect on Facebook. Once you do this, you are one new contact closer to your first Restaurant Invasion.

Three of them, attending seven events in one week, developed 210 new contacts (new acquaintances or Facebook friends). Each individual succeeded in capturing roughly 10 contacts per event.

When all 200 people were contacted, and invited to an event we hosted, only 100 showed up, roughly 50%— but many of them brought a friend! When it was all tallied, over 200 people showed up when we counted their friends who also attended. That's a significant number!

What this means is that if you attend a MeetUp.com event every day, all by yourself, for a month, you will likely secure 250-300 new contacts that you can invite to your events. And that's all you need to get your business launched. If you had just 25 people attend your first Restaurant Invasion I would consider it a success and a great first step towards a successful new business.

Here are some tips to maximize your success when you attend a MeetUp.com event.

1. Always, always, always, get to know the event organizer. Chances are, this is not their first MeetUp event, and they probably know the most people. You want to invite that person, the event organizer, to your Restaurant Invasion because that person likely has the most friends.

2. MeetUp.com has a lot of food centric events available. If you attend these in pursuit of new

contacts, chances are good that the people you meet will be interested in your Restaurant Invasion. Even if you don't attend food specific MeetUp events, everybody eats. You'll still be fine, don't worry!

3. Your goal is to meet and befriend 20 MeetUp event organizers. Again, this is because MeetUp event organizers usually know the most people. If you invite 20 event organizers and each one brings five people to your first event, you'll have 100 people. Not a bad start. Event organizers are gold. Meet them, exchange contact information, and nurture those relationships.

4. If you're still a little nervous about how to network at these events that you attend, re-read the section on F.O.R.M., that talks more about the specifics of networking.

5. MeetUp.com is not the only site where you can learn about events to attend where you can meet people. Try Craigslist.com and look at the casting call events. If there's a casting call for movie extras you might be able to get a part in the next big blockbuster. That means you'll likely be mingling with hundreds of other movie extras, who might respond to invitations for events.

6. Local trade shows are a great place to go to find large groups of people, especially job seeking and college fair types of trade shows. There are any number of other categories on Craigslist, and other websites, where you can learn about events and where you'll meet a lot of people.

7. Toastmasters is a club that meets in virtually every city in America where people, who have an interest in public speaking, join to practice public speaking. If you join a Toastmasters group, you are sure to meet a group of 20 or 30 people, who come together once a month or so to give speeches to each other. This organization hosts chapter-level events with even more people where local groups come together for speaking contests and meetings.

8. Active.com is a website that posts groups who get together for various outdoor active events like running, biking, team sports, even marathon events. If this is your thing, try showing up at these events, making friends and asking for people's Facebook details.

9. There are business and community groups you can join including Rotary Groups, Kiwanis, local Chambers Of Commerce groups. Every town has one, two, or five of these.

10. Try this Google search: "groups to join" or "clubs to join" or "social clubs" or "membership clubs"

11. There are apps that help you to meet new people in group settings including: MeetMyDog, Nearify, Foursquare, CitySocializer, EventBrite, Gravy, Time To Enjoy, Supper Club (It's food related: Bonus points!), Peoplehunt, and of course MeetUp.com has an app.

12. If you're religious, join a church group. Many of the non-denominational Christian churches have all

kinds of groups from Bible Study to special interest and friendship groups.

13. If you find any gold mines that I haven't mentioned, please email me at HsuMJames@gmail.com and tell me about them.

So you don't know anybody to invite to your Restaurant Invasion? Not for long. Remember, everybody who started this business started somewhere, either with a few friends or a bunch of friends. Very few people who get started in this business had a contact list as large as mine. But if you're creative and willing to work for your own success, there are many simple ways to meet different people. And your life will be richer for the effort you put into growing your connections.

Please allow me to get philosophical for a moment: Life is about relationships. Whether you know it or not, your life is about relationships. Your happiness (or lack of it) in your job probably has a lot to do with how well you get along with your boss and whether or not he/she is fair and kind to you. Your happiness in your marriage is, or will, have everything to do with the quality of your relationship with your husband or wife. Your happiness in your leisure time will have everything to do with the quality of your relationships with the five or six people you spend the most time with. Your happiness with your family likely has a lot to do with the quality of the relationships you have with them.

Your life is really the sum, or total, of your relationships. This business, and your willingness to expand your universe of contacts, will shape your life, will improve your life, and may even save your life. Because ultimately, some of the people you meet on this journey will become dear friends. Remember someone without strong relationships, is dead or dying.

There are very few people who don't know anyone, and have zero friends. You read about these kinds of people after they commit some atrocity or suicide. Relationships are your life—they are life itself. And the skills and relationships you gather while mastering this business will make your life bigger, sweeter, and more powerful.

I challenge you to meet 100 new people in the next 30 days—just 3 to 4 new people a day. I promise if you do, your life will never be the same. And, if you're working this business and growing your universe of relationships, your income is likely to improve just as fast.

So now you've built and expanded your cell phone list, we'll look at what actually happens at the Restaurant Invasion.

Chapter 6

How to Conduct the Restaurant Invasion

In this chapter, I'll show you how to actually conduct a Restaurant Invasion. You've texted everyone the day before to remind them, and you have your head count. Let's assume that 50% arrive early, 20% arrive on time, 20% arrive 15 minutes late, and 10% flake on you.

Dealing with those who don't show up

You'll find that one issue you can't avoid are the people who flake. There will be particular individuals who will confirm the day before and just won't show. They may tell you a family member ran away, they had a car accident, or had to go to the hospital. I've heard it all. Literally an hour into your Restaurant Invasion, the person who flaked is on Instagram showing off the party they are at, yet they haven't texted you back and won't answer their phone. Don't take it personally—that's just how people are and it's the way it is. Although it's tempting, **do not burn that bridge!** Be nice, and invite them to the next one. It doesn't matter, as this wasn't a one and done for you. It's something you're going to be hosting weekly or even daily!

When people arrive

Show up to the restaurant earlier than your guests do! Get there in plenty of time for those who are early. As people arrive, make sure you introduce yourself right away—**do not wait!**

- **Do not** allow 1 second of awkwardness.
- **Do not** forget to immediately introduce 1 person to another.
- **Do not** allow 1 person to feel uninvited—this is not high school.
- **Do not** allow 1 person to feel left out of the conversation.

Look out for people who are arriving as guests of your friends, the people that you don't know. You'll spot them because they probably look lost, or are looking down at their phone.

At Restaurant Invasions, your number 1 goal is to: **MAKE EVERYONE FEEL COMFORTABLE.**

Get your table. It might be a huge, long table or the group may be divided up into many small tables depending on the restaurant.

Rules of the invasion

You are now the host of this event that *you are hosting*. So remember these simple host rules.

- Your job is **not** to have a seat at a certain table.
- Your job is to be the best host in the entire history of hosts.

- Never sit, or stand, and have a conversation at one certain table for more than 5-10 minutes.
- When others are talking, look around at everyone, smile and see who's paying attention and who's not, and involve others in the conversation.
- Talk to your friends who are there, but the important part is to make friends with those that you don't know yet.

First round: Meeting people

The easiest way to start the process of getting to know everyone is to start collecting your database. Don't forget, collecting your database is key to your future success in this business. You'll want to collect their first and last names, phone number, and an email. Basically, anyway you can connect with them, so that you can invite them to future Restaurant Invasions. Once everyone is seated, take out your smartphone, pull up your Notes app, and ask everyone to input their information. Have the first few lines pre-written out as an example for others to follow. You'll hand your phone to your guests and ask them to input their information. People sometimes feel weird if they don't see any other names, so help them feel comfortable and start it off. If you can, have 3-5 people you already know pre-fill their information.

Example

James Hsu
7021234567
hsumjames@gmail.com

Ashley Chau
7021234567
Ashley@mpmvsm.com

Tracy Wong
7029876543
Tracy@mpmvsm.com

When you approach a table, you will probably already know at least one person sitting there. If for some reason, the way the seating worked means you don't know anyone because they're all friends of friends, then that's fine.

Make an announcement to the table:

"Hey guys, If we haven't met yet, my names is James Hsu. Thank you so much for coming to our little event. I know you guys will love the food. We do these Restaurant Invasions on a regular basis and I would love to personally invite you guys to future events."

Then hand the phone over to the person who's smiling, looking at you, not awkward, and say:

"All you guys have to do is fill this out. I would love to text you for future events if you are interested."

Once the first person starts, the majority will fill it out.

Second round: Checking in

Once this is finished, go around again for the second time and now start with one of the following:

- How's the menu look?
- What'd you guys get to drink?
- Has anyone ever eaten here before?
- Can anyone recommend anything specific?
- How do you guys know each other?
- How do you know Frederick (the friend that brought them)?
- What does everyone do for work?
- Does anyone go to school?

These simple conversations should be around 5-10 minutes. Once this is done and everyone has spoken, your job is to move to the next table or the next group of friends.

"Well, nice to meet everyone. I'm gonna go and say hi to everyone else, then I'll be back."

You repeat this process with every table.

Third round: Be the server

When you get to the same table again for the third rotation, your next set of questions should be:

- What'd everyone end up getting?
- Is there anything I can get anyone? (drink refills if you're allowed to, napkins, straws, etc.)

You are basically a part-time server, making sure that all your guests have everything they need and, most importantly, ensuring that they are having a good time.

Fourth round: Remember something about them

Try to remember the conversations you've had with each table. Remember their names, and something about where they are from, or something interesting they said in the other rotations, such as a vacation they are about to take. Ask them something specific about them so the entire table can hear the story. For example:

"Hey guys, everyone good? Great. So, Frederick, tell me about the trip to New York you are about to go on. Just by yourself? Family? Girlfriend? What are you going for?"

Listen to the story. Move on to the next table. Your goal is to become likeable, friendly, entertaining, and, most importantly, for them to leave this dinner saying: "That was fun, I met a lot of friendly people and had a good meal."

That way, when you follow up the next day, the only thing they are thinking when you ask them "Can I invite you to future events?" is "Yes, of course!"

Chapter 7

SINALOA – Your Secret to Success

As you've seen, the concept behind the Restaurant Invasion is simple and it sounds like a great way to get paid to eat, which it is. But I also need to be honest with you. There will be rejection. In this chapter, I'll explain what happens when you're rejected and how to develop the mindset to overcome that.

What to do when restaurants say no

When you're approaching restaurant owners or managers, no matter how great the *Restaurant Invasion* concept sounds—some of them just won't go for it. Not everybody will buy into your idea, and not everyone will participate. It's important that you understand *you are not harming their business by asking*. You are helping businesses find new loyal customers and creating fun outings with your friends. If one business doesn't want to work with you, you can always try another one. You haven't lost anything by asking, but they have lost the potential for acquiring new customers, Yelp reviews, etc.

The one thing that keeps most people from succeeding is the fear of rejection. Don't let fear get in your way of

73

making a 6-figure income. Imagine pitching your idea, and a restaurant owner says, "*No.*" What is the worst that can happen? You've probably guessed it—**absolutely nothing**! If someone says *no* to you, you simply move on to the next restaurant. Don't get discouraged, and do not give up. Remember, there's no harm in asking. We simply proceed to the next restaurant until one says, "*Yes!*"

There is one basic principle you need to understand in order to overcome all fears of rejection. That principle is SINALOA. We're not talking about the town in Mexico, but rather an acronym. S.I.N.A.L.O.A—**S**afety **I**n **N**umbers **A**nd **L**aw **O**f **A**verages.

The best way to understand SINALOA is through dating. Let's say that I'm single and looking to find myself a girlfriend. I muster up the courage to ask a girl out on a date, and she rejects me. I, now, have one of two options. I can, one, give up on women altogether and never ask another girl out for the rest of my life. Or, two, I can try again until I find someone who will agree to going out with me. SINALOA is just that—trying again and again, until you get the result you're looking for. It's all about knowing your ratio.

The formula for this ratio is simple. For this example, it's the number of women who agree to going out on a date with you divided by the total number of women you've asked out.

Let's break it down further. The phrase *Safety In Numbers* means the more women I ask out, the higher the chances are of getting a date. As a result, the more dates I go on, the greater the chances of finding a girlfriend.

The best way to illustrate **Law Of A**verages is by giving you an example. Let's say, every 25 women I spoke to, I would get only one to agree to go out with me. My ratio would then be 1 (women who agree to going out with me) out of 25 (total women asked). So, if I wanted to make sure I went on 2 dates this week, I would then have to make sure I spoke to at least 50 women to ensure I get 2 dates. Business is no different. It's about increasing your ratio (your **Law Of A**verages) by speaking to more people.

Applying SINALOA to business

When applying SINALOA to Restaurant Invasions, you must speak to many different businesses **every single day**. Remember, *Safety In Numbers*—The more businesses you talk to, the more likely you will succeed. Don't set your sights on one specific restaurant and get disappointed if they end up saying no.

Once rejected, most people will have the mindset of quitting, telling themselves: *This will never work! What was I thinking*? But by applying SINALOA, and understanding both **S**afety **I**n **N**umbers **A**nd the **L**aw **O**f **A**verages, this is the first step to getting the right mindset and heading down the path to success. By knowing your ratio, you'll know exactly how many businesses you need to talk to in order to get the results you want.

Once you get the first restaurant to buy into the idea, you start building your confidence, and this business becomes very easy. When you're in a restaurant, surrounded by your friends, having a good time, making money, and knowing you are helping businesses succeed, it's a great feeling. Most businesses will need to *see it to believe it*. By seeing the new customers you're bringing in, and seeing their business become relevant on social media, the Restaurant Invasion concept becomes a no-brainer. Especially, considering the restaurant owners didn't pay any upfront money for advertising.

Generally, restaurant owners know other restaurant owners, and if the owner of Joe's New York Pizza is happy with the experience, you should be able to ask for referrals. You can ask them, *"Hey, do you know any other restaurants, that aren't competing with you, that might be interested in doing this?"* You will definitely get other clients this way.

Remember that whenever someone says *"no,"* you're that much closer to the person who will say *"yes"*. Don't be discouraged when someone says no, and don't give up, even if your ratio is low. Michael Jordan, possibly the greatest basketball player of all time, had a field goal percentage of a little under 50%. That's crazy when you think that he got paid $30 million in one season with the Chicago Bulls, even when he missed more than half of his shots.

Knowing your ratios

Knowing your ratios doesn't just mean knowing how many restaurants say yes versus how many say no. This also applies to your restaurant invaders as well. For every event take note of the following:

- How many people showed up vs. how many invited
- How many people flaked (make note of who)
- How many people showed up on time
- Average Bill

- Your cut

For example:

Invasion 1: Joe's NY Pizza
- Invited 50; 35 showed up (Show-up Ratio: 35/50 = 70%)
- 25 flaked (Flaked Ratio: 25/70 = 30%)
- 30 on time (On time Ratio: 30/35 = 85%)
- Average bill turned out to be: $30/person = $750
- 50% for me would be: $375

Invasion 2: Carlos 'N Charlie's
- Invited 100; 75 showed up (Show-up Ratio: 75/100 = 75%)
- 25 flaked (Flaked Ratio: 25/100 = 25%)
- 67 on time (On time Ratio: 67/75 = 89%)
- Average bill turned out to be: $30/person = $2,250
- 50% for me would be: $1,125

Note that taking the average of your *show-up ratio* is extremely important, as this will give you an idea of how many people you need to invite in order to hit the desired number of invaders you've promised for your next Restaurant Invasions.

Once you do at least five invasions, you'll be able to look at all your numbers and be able to forecast and control how much money you make.

Let's say you want to make $10,000 a month. You know that your average show-up ratio is 70%, meaning 7/10 people will attend your event when you invite them. So, you just have to figure how many invasions you need to do this month to make $10,000.

If you need to generate $20,000 in receipts/meal tickets for the restaurants in order for you to earn $10,000, simply break down your numbers:

- If each meal averaged $30/person; $20,000 divided by $30 means that 667 people will need to eat with you this month
- 667 people divided by 30 days means you need 22 people to eat with you every day for the entire month.

If you average a 70% show-up ratio:
- 22 people divided by 70% means that you need to invite minimum 32 people a day to eat with you.
- If you invite 32 people a day to dinner, 22 people would show up
- 22 people spending $30 on dinner would be $660 in business, 50% is yours: $330 a day in business x 30 days would make you $9,900 a month

Once you have an idea of what your ratios are, you will be able to dictate how much money you earn every month. Just calculate all your numbers on how many restaurant owners you need to talk to every day, and figure out how many people you need to eat with you on a daily basis.

The important point behind this is that if you master your craft and have the right mindset, there is an unlimited amount of money you can make for yourself. You can eat your way to a 6-figure income, just by mastering the concept of SINALOA.

In the next chapter, we'll look at the power of Yelp, as it is a great way to grow your reputation and convince more restaurant owners why they should take part!

Chapter 8

How to Harness the Power of Yelp

If Yelp isn't a popular app in your country, there should be at least one app where you can write food reviews for restaurants, such as TripAdvisor or Google My Business. The principles can be applied to other review sites. But, since most people are familiar with Yelp, I'll use it as an example in this chapter.

How Yelp works

Yelp can have a huge impact on businesses, both positive and negative. Yelp encourages people to tell the truth about a business; if a business has bad reviews on Yelp, then it is bad, and if it has good reviews, then it is good. There have been horror stories of businesses that have gone bankrupt and even closed just because of bad reviews on Yelp. On the other hand, Yelp can boost an unknown business into stardom if there are lots of great reviews.

To use Yelp to its fullest potential, you need to understand the principles of it. Yelp will hide a review until the reviewer demonstrates that they're not just bashing or praising one or two businesses. So, if you download the

Yelp app and never check in to restaurants, and leave a 5-star review for one restaurant, Yelp will not rank that review highly, and may even hide that review.

Here is how it works, the more reviews you write, the higher your reviews will rank. The reason Yelp works this way is because they don't want competing businesses to simply create accounts to bash their competition or praise themselves. This system ensures that people are honest.

Build your Yelp credibility

With that in mind, you need to start building your credibility on the Yelp app. Show other Yelp users that you are a "real" person. Add a real profile photo, take advantage of Yelp coupons, and really use the app. Check in, post photos, add friends, and write reviews every day.

When you go to a restaurant, check in and take photos. Leave detailed reviews with a lot of "meat". This means you should never say things like *"This place sucks! I'm never going back again!"* Instead, leave a thorough review about what you ate, the experience, the environment, the restrooms, how clean it is, and so on. Leaving honest reviews of businesses will make your Yelp account much more valuable. Ensure that you follow Yelp's terms of service to create a respected account.

By doing this, you will gain badges and more notoriety in the Yelp community. You'll be surprised that the more you use Yelp, the more clout you have with the Yelp community. You may even become an "Elite." Elite writers are more trusted than regular reviewers because they write the most reviews, and they always give a honest assessment of a business. This will help your emerging Restaurant Invasion business.

Use Yelp to your advantage

Once you have gained notoriety on Yelp, you can use this to convince restaurant owners to host a Restaurant Invasion. When pitching to restaurant owners, you can show them the app as an example. This proves your clout to potential clients—they can see that after you've checked-in at a restaurant and left a review, the review shows up higher because you are a trusted source.

Another way to use Yelp to your advantage is asking your friends who have Yelp to leave reviews. Then, you can tell the restaurant owners that your friends who use Yelp will also check in and write fair reviews of their experience.

More importantly, never promise "good reviews" to restaurant owners. It is not your job to provide "good" reviews for any business, and this is something that the business needs to understand. You are giving them an opportunity to impress Yelp contributors by offering great customer service and amazing food, not to automatically give them positive reviews.

Building an Elite Yelp group

Another benefit of Yelp is that you can even use it to make new friends. To increase your popularity in the community, give other Yelp writers "compliments." Befriend them on Yelp, and you can then build a list of Elite Yelpers to invite to your events. Imagine how a business will feel if you tell them you are going to invite

15 Elite Yelpers intermixed with regular guests. They should be thrilled.

The potential of multiple Elite Yelpers leaving reviews will make your Restaurant Invasions even more enticing—and the business owners will see the added value of using your events for promotional marketing.

So, you should understand how Yelp will help build your network and add significant value to your Restaurant Invasions, making it more appealing to business owners. Now, we need to go over one of the most critical aspects of this business: the hustle.

Chapter 9:

Always Hustle

So far, you've seen how simple the concept of getting paid to eat is, and how much fun you'll have doing it. But, if you want to make a six-figure income from Restaurant Invasions, then you have to put in the work. Using this concept, you can make anywhere from a thousand dollars to a six-figure income. The difference between these two amounts is how much you are willing to hustle. If you want to make a million dollars, hustling is a non-negotiable and non-debatable aspect. So, in this chapter, I'll explain the importance of the hustle.

Hustle every day

Every night before you go to bed, get prepared by mapping out which 10 restaurants you'll walk into the next morning. Make sure you visit the restaurants before they get busy, so Google their opening hours the day before. If they open at 11:00 am, get there when they open, or maybe a little beforehand—when the employees, manager, or owner arrive to prep for the day.

If you want to be successful in starting this business, you're need to be strategic. If you have a full-time job, this may mean moving your lunch hour around in order to visit the target restaurant when you're most likely to meet the owners, often between the hours of 11 am and 1 pm. I suggest asking your supervisor if you can take an early lunch every other day, and eat in the car while you're driving to the different restaurants you hope to target.

In business, a true hustler is consistent. This means you need to talk to a minimum of 10 new restaurants a day, **every day**. Don't walk into 20 restaurants in one day and then skip the next two or three days. Although it's tempting to visit 20 restaurants in a day, as the day goes on, you'll become more and more sloppy because you are tired.

You need to stop pitching when your energy level is low, because people will see that and interpret the lack of energy as a lack of enthusiasm for their business. When you give yourself a finite number of clients to see, you'll be better prepared for each meeting—you'll know what they are selling, hone your pitch, and have more energy to explain what you are doing.

You'll also notice that by putting yourself on a schedule and being consistent, it will also give you better habits in life. You begin to build self-awareness. Having structure in your life provides great benefits. For example, you can exercise like a maniac for 5 hours in the gym one day, but it won't give you the results you are looking for overall. Ask any personal trainer whether you should work out for 5 hours once a week or 1 hour every day for 5 days— they'll say the latter.

Don't eat at places that don't support you

This may sound harsh, but it's vital that you understand a few things. First, this is a business, and you are here to make money. Secondly, this is a business, and you are adding nothing but value to the business owners.

From this day forward, if you a pitch a business and they don't give you the time to even explain what you do **never** go to that business again.

I'm not saying all businesses have to host a Restaurant Invasion, but if they won't give you the time of day to hear you out, do **not** support their business.

Put your time and money into places that also want to support you. There's so many options to choose from, why wouldn't you only eat at places that support you and are willing to see the value you bring to the table.

Being consistent and making a routine

Want to make six-figures? Let's be realistic, you need to work every day. But, if you enjoy what you're doing, it won't feel like work. You'll discover that you love eating out with new people and you'll love that people want to be around you. If you want to be in the top 1%-5% of American money-earners, you have to hustle: head-down, tail-up, run-with-the-ball.

What if you talk to ten businesses a day and you only get one business to agree? Once you've hosted an invasion at a restaurant, assuming it was a success and well attended, chances are the owner will be open to another event. Simply ask them if he'd like to do this again next month or week. In most cases, the restaurant owners will say yes. So if the business is having you come in every day of the week, you are making new friends on social media, and you continuously pack the restaurant, day in and day out, you will be making a generous amount of income.

But you **will** get new clients, probably at least one new client every day. You will gain clients due to the number of the people you'll be talking to daily (remember SINALOA). You just need to talk to a minimum of 10 new businesses a day, which is 300 a month, and as long as you're doing that, you'll succeed.

Also, once you start doing this, all of these new friends you are meeting will have friends who own other restaurants, bars, and clubs. They'll start asking you *"Would you hold an event like this at my friend's place?"* Or *"The owner is my friend, can I give them your number?"* It's remarkable how hosting an entertaining event that people value will lead to new introductions, not just socially, but to prospective business owners.

All of this might sound overwhelming, but after you've completed one invasion, and then do this over and over, it starts to become a routine. You might have an event every day. Once you're in a routine, having two invasions in one day won't be too difficult. People eat breakfast, lunch, and dinner every day, so you could have three invasions a day if you felt able to manage it!

Even if you succeed at holding one or two events a week, it will be extra cash for you, and you can increase as much or as little as you feel comfortable. Whatever you're doing will become comfortable and your routine will become more consistent.

Increasing your business

Believe it or not, it's easy to build your list from eating with 5 friends to eating with 500. It's all about database collecting. Even if you only have 5 friends, ask all 5 of those friends to do you a favor and bring one friend with them the first time.

So, your 5 friends each bring a friend. That's 5 new names, 5 new Facebook friends, 5 new email addresses, 5 new phone numbers. At the next event, you have 10 people who went to your first event, had fun, loved the environment, and loved **you**! So, these 10 friends each bring another friend, which makes 10 more new people. At the next event, the new people each bring another person, and so on.

If you do one event a week—so four events a month, then 3 months later, you will have had 12 events. You will have a new database of people you normally never would have met, but now, you'll starting bonding with these people and expanding your network at the same time.

Do this process for 6 months to a year, and you will have an entirely new circle of friends. Some of them will look forward to your Restaurant Invasions, so if you give them a heads up, they will always be there. Do this long enough over the course of a year, and you'll have a guaranteed number of regulars. Then, all you have to do is keep building your database to get more regulars.

You'll also find that as your business grows, other people will become teammates, because they love what you do. They'll start to say, *"Hey, if I bring friends, can I eat for free, too?"* Suddenly, they'll be bringing 10 people and splitting the profits with you. You'll be sharing the money and arranging these events together.

That's when this concept becomes even more fun, because you'll have people coming with you to events, and you'll be making new friends, and meeting people you never thought you'd meet. All of this while eating for free and making a six-figure income.

Also, this all doesn't stop at restaurants. Once you start making a solid income, held really successful invasions, and really mastered the art of databasing, you can expand to different kinds of events. You can then take your organization/business to the next level.

Because you are the one that now puts things together, people will associate you with a good time. Anything that you want put together, invite your database because they are used to you inviting them to places, and having a wonderful time.

For example, while I was mentoring different individuals, I realized a few of them were all artists, looking to display their work in an art show. So, what did I do? I held my own private art show. My students were able to sell and display their art because I invited 200 people from my database. I created a totally new event.

I went on and hosted private concerts, featuring a bunch of local musicians.

Once you mastered the techniques of mobilizing people and building a database, you have a following that will go almost anywhere with you.

The most important part to any business is traffic and that's what you do!

Now that we've discussed how hustling will expand your database, which means more people you'll have to bring to your events, it's time I show you the technical side of database collecting.

Chapter 10

Database Collecting

To increase your business, you'll need to increase your database or your network of contacts. One of the most efficient ways to accomplish this is through database collecting at your Restaurant Invasions. So in this chapter, I'll show you the art of collecting people's information. The best time to do this is while your guests are checking in (or getting settled) at the start of the event. Remember holding an invasion and not collecting a database of contacts is **wasting** an opportunity for the next event.

Checking your guests in

I'll base this tutorial on iPhones and iPads, but other phones have similar apps you can use. The first thing we'll walk through is the Notes app. Before the event, you have a headcount of who is due to attend. So after the event, you need to know who actually showed up. When the numbers are low like 5, it's easy to recall who came, but when the numbers are closer to 100, it's hard to remember. For instance, I once had 3,318 people come to watch a movie with me. So, to ensure that I can capture all of the data I have everyone check in.

As you recall in Chapter 6, the **most** important thing for you to do is capture people's first and last names, phone numbers, and email addresses. Keeping a database of this information is how you'll get in touch with them in the future.

It's best to do the check-in on an iPad. If you use your phone, it looks unprofessional. If you use a laptop, it's heavy and you have to carry it around and worry about it during the event. An iPad, tablet, or similar device is easy to keep track of, lightweight, and looks professional. You could use a clipboard and paper if you don't have an iPad, but be warned that it can be difficult to read the information later due to people's handwriting.

Keeping track of your guests

To start, you should always create a file for each restaurant, such as "Joe's New York Pizza". When using your iPad (or tablet), the note will also have the time and date of the recorded information. Beyond that, it's important to track these five pieces of information:

1. Date of the event
2. Time of the event
3. Number of attendees
4. Attendee information
5. How much you earned

Again, as I mentioned in Chapter 6, I always have the first few lines pre-written out as an example for others to follow.

Joe's New York Pizza
Wednesday, April 11, 2018 (current head count)

James Hsu
702-123-4567
JamesHsu@gmail.com

Ashley
702-123-4567
Ashley@gmail.com

Tracy
702-123-4567
Tracy@gmail.com

Chasing
702-123-4567
Chasing@gmail.com

Cyndi
702-123-4567
Cyndi@gmail.com

Aaron
702-123-4567
Aaron@gmail.com

Song
702-123-4567
Song@gmail.com

Kent
702-123-4567
Kent@gmail.com

Clark
702-123-4567
Clark@gmail.com

Then at the event, I say to each person, *"Thanks for coming to our Restaurant Invasion. I'd like to invite you to future Restaurant Invasions around Las Vegas. Would you be interested?"* 99% of the time they'll say, *"Yeah, sure."*

Then, I hand them my iPad and they fill the form in. It's imperative to get not only their first and last name, but to get their email address, and phone number.

Keep an eye on the form. Most people fill out forms without really paying attention to what it says. They often base their answers on what the previous person wrote, so if someone doesn't include part of their information, such as their phone number or email address if they don't have one, then the next person might miss this too.

If you see someone do this, fix it by pasting this line further back on the list, or move a full entry below it. If you hand the list to the next person without checking it, they'll base their information on the last entry and you may not get all the information you wanted. For example:

Database Collection Form

Joe's New York Pizza
Wednesday, April 11, 2018 (current head count)

James Hsu
702-123-4567
JamesHsu@gmail.com

Ashley
702-123-4567
Ashley@gmail.com

Tracy
Tracy@gmail.com   ← Incomplete

Chasing
Chasing@gmail.com   ← Incomplete

Cyndi
702-123-4567
Cyndi@gmail.com

Aaron
702-123-4567
Aaron@gmail.com

Song
702-123-4567
Song@gmail.com

What to do with this information

Once the event has finished, you will have all the new information on your Notes app. Before you do anything else, I recommend taking the entire database and transferring (copy and paste) it to a Microsoft Word document, or any word processing document. Like this:

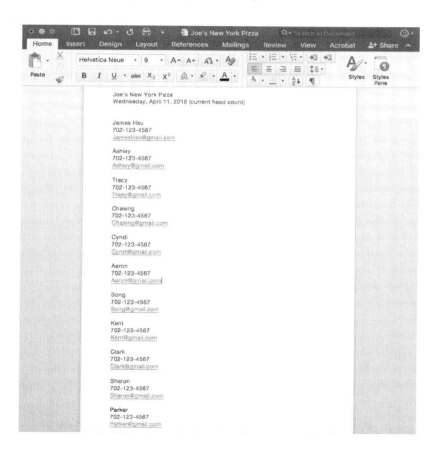

Then, you will go through the database manually, adding each number to your phone. Once you've added their contact information, that's when you will send your follow-up text (which is covered later in this chapter). After you've done this, delete the name and phone number for each contact. This will leave only their emails:

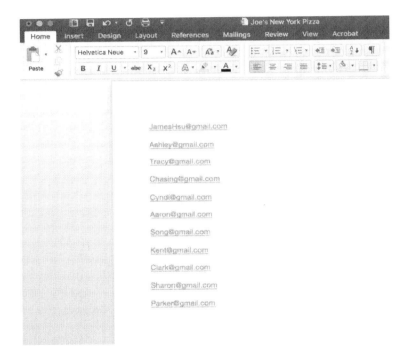

Later on, you are going to email all of these individuals with a thank you email (which I'll go over in Chapter 12). However, you still need to store this information. Now, take this current list of emails and save them to a folder.

You will first create a folder titled "Emails." Then, save this document as "Database 1" or simply, "Database," with only their emails to that folder. After your next event, go through the same process, but add those new emails back to this document. Continue doing this until you have no more than 400 emails. You are going to stop at that number because Gmail doesn't allow you to email more than 500 people per day. If you don't use Gmail, you'll have to test the limit for your email service (Yahoo, Hotmail, etc.) yourself. I personally use Gmail because it's incredibly effective, so I'll be referring to it for email examples. So, while the minor details might vary, the big picture remains the same no matter what email service you use.

Again, I'll go over more information about emailing in Chapter 12, we are just focusing on saving this information.

Once you've acquired around 400, you will start a new document, "Database 2". Copy and paste 400 new emails into that document, so on, and so forth.

Eventually, the "Emails" folder will look like this:

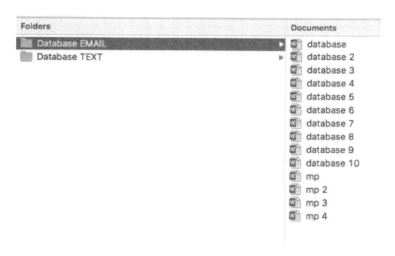

Now, you will have easy, instant access to all of these emails.

Contacting your new contacts

Now, you should already be planning for the next event. The success of the next event, however, will depend on how many new contacts you have made. *Why*? Because, you can't keep bringing in the same people, over and over, to the same restaurant and expect the business to see the value.

If you have a database of 100 names, phone numbers, and email addresses, that will only go so far. You're either growing your business or you're letting your business slowly die. You can make money or make excuses. When you have a database, your goal is to add names, numbers, and email addresses every single day. **Remember** to add 10 new friends on Facebook every day to get those 10 new numbers as well.

So, it's time to text your new contacts and turn them into potential future restaurant invaders. There's a rule when contacting people—**thank your new contacts the very next day**. Do **not** break this rule. If the Restaurant Invasion was at lunchtime today, then text them tomorrow at lunchtime. If the event was breakfast on Monday, text them Tuesday morning. If the event was dinner today, send your text tomorrow late-afternoon.

If you text everyone within the 24-hour time frame, everyone will remember you. From experience, I've texted people 48 hours after an event and some of them have responded saying, *"Who is this?"* because they've forgotten. To most people, the Restaurant Invasion is just a bunch of friends having dinner. This is why you should follow-up within 24 hours.

The follow-up text

In your Notes app, save a file as "Restaurant Invasions: Thank You Text." For the body of the text, the wording will be generic, such as, *"James Hsu here. Thank you for coming with us to Joe's New York Pizza! Would it be okay with you if I invited you to future events?"* However, when you're texting a new contact to say thanks—you need to make it personal by adding the person's name.

If you have a lot of people to thank, open the Notes app, select "Restaurant Invasions: Thank You Text", "Select" the entire text message, and press "Copy." Go through your "Database Collection" document, and grab the phone numbers one by one. Invite the individual by selecting their phone number link, and press "Send Message." Make it custom by typing their name at the beginning of the text, adding a personal touch. **Do** this for each of the new contacts from that Restaurant Invasion.

Once they've given the go-ahead for you to text them about the next event, send them your personal, and social media, information. This is because you want them to follow you on Twitter, Instagram, and Facebook, and subscribe to your YouTube channel if you have one. The person will see your social media handles and will get the impression that you're a professional, which adds to your credibility.

I personally also include a link to my book, <u>Mobilizing People</u>, on Amazon to add even more credibility, because the person doesn't know that I'm an author. The likelihood is that they know nothing about me—just that I'm a friend of whoever invited them.

After you've texted each and every person who attended, and they've said "yes" to future events, you can add them to your mass texting app and the list of people you are allowed to mass text.

Mass texting app? Yes! This is going to be one of the most important tools you'll use to make your business a success. As your list grows, it's going to get harder and harder to text your database members individually—thus, the mass texting app comes into play.

Chapter 11

How to Use the Mass Texting App

In this chapter, I'll show you how to use a mass texting app. I'll be using MassTextMessage.com as an example, but the specific app is not important, just the concept. I should mention that this application is an Apple product, but Android devices have apps that are similar. Start by downloading the app, or a similar app, and click on the icon to launch it.

A mass texting app is a godsend, because once you start creating groups of people to text, you never have to go back to sending individual texts. As your events begin to compound you're really going to have an unlimited database of people, so you won't have time to text everyone individually.

Carrier throttling

When mass texting, there is an issue you need to be aware of—carrier throttling. If you text too many people too fast, your carrier will "throttle" you and cut off your text messaging. The app will allow you to send as many texts as you like, but if you try to send more than I'm suggesting, you'll risk carrier throttling. I've experienced this problem with the AT&T, Sprint, Verizon, and T-Mobile cell services. When this happens, the person won't receive your message because your carrier will have disabled your sending ability.

Carrier throttling can cause a huge problem, so include yourself in each text group, so you can confirm that your message went out to everybody. I ensure that my groups have no more than 11 people in them. Each group has 10 phone numbers of contacts, plus my own phone number so I know they've received it because I have. If I don't receive the text, I can deduce that none of the other 10 received it either.

The list in my mass text app has 50 groups with 10 people each (not including myself). That makes a total of 500 people that I mass text directly about an event.

Creating a group

To create a new group in the app, press the "+" symbol at the top of the screen. Name the group after the last one you added, so if the last one was "49", this one will be "50." Add yourself using the "+" symbol, then your name and number will appear on screen. Add the other contacts and their numbers—remember no more than 10 per group (excluding your own).

This might take a while, so be patient. The more numbers you have, the longer it will take. However, it's worth it because you will save yourself time in the long run. Also, you'll notice that people communicate better through texting, and will reply faster than they would to an email.

Sending a mass text

Now, you can use this application to invite your database to future events or invasions. To write messages, again I use the Notes app on my iPhone, and a create a new note called "Mass Text for (event/restaurant)." Then, write out the message you want to send to everyone.

I'll use a recent event as an example. Remember, the bigger your database, the more people you'll have to invite to events, the more people will like you, the more money you'll make, and the more successful your future events will be. Here's the template below:

"Art and Fashion Show! FREE! 6:00 pm-8:30 pm, Sun., Oct. 18. I'm hosting! Inside F45 Training. 1000 S. Rampart 89145. Behind Boca Park, behind Wendy's! RSVP: can you come?"

I sent the text on Monday and the show is on Sunday. Around 150 people replied, so about 100-150 will actually show up. After the event, I add the new numbers to the database, which will probably be an additional 70 numbers. This will bring us up to number "58" or "59" in the mass text app.

The mass text app only costs around $2.99 from the App Store, but it's worth the investment. At the end of the day it will save you time and make you lots of money!

Now, that you've mastered texting your database, let's go over emailing them!

Chapter 12

Emailing Your Database

So, we've gone over how to use a mass texting application to contact your database through their phone numbers—but what about their email? Emailing your database is just as critical as texting them.

Emailing new people

Every time I meet someone new, I send them a generic email through Gmail. I enter one of the new email addresses and enter the "Subject" such as *"Joe's New York Pizza Event."*

In the body of the email, I'll say

"Kent: Thank you for coming to our event at Joe's New York Pizza! We had a lot of fun. We hope you also had a lot of fun."

I ensure my name and social media information is already saved at the bottom of the email.

If more than 10 people show up to a restaurant, you might be able to send a carbon copy (Cc) to everybody, but it wouldn't have their name on it. If you sent a blind carbon copy (Bcc), it also wouldn't be personalized, plus it would probably go to their spam folder. You have a better chance of the email not going to spam if it's been addressed with their name. But, if you're doing invasions with large numbers of people, you might want to send them a mass email anyway.

Once I've sent the email, if I have their phone number as well, I'll also text them a few days later. The text would say, *"Hi, Kent. Just want to make sure you got my email I sent you. Thank you again for coming to our invasion. I had a lot of fun."* Hopefully, they'll then check their email.

Using a flyer email

So, I'll pull up an email database, select all and copy, and close the database. I go back to Gmail, select "Compose", go to "Bcc", and "Paste" (if you have a lot of email addresses in this database, it will take a while to load), "Bcc" yourself to ensure you receive it, enter the subject and event information, and press "Send."

For example, your subject might be *"Restaurant Invasions for the month of August 2018. Hope you can make it!"* Then, copy-and-paste some flyer text into the email. Below is a flyer email that I've used, so feel free to copy it and use it. All you have to do is fill in the restaurant name, time/date, and location.

Hey, FOODIES!!!

*It's that time again for our next **Restaurant Invasion**!*

*Come and join me, along with other foodies in town, to try the delicious food at (**RESTAURANT NAME[S]**)*

Below are details for this month's Restaurant Invasions:

(Restaurant Name)
(Date, Time)
(Location)
TEXT ME @ (Phone Number) to RSVP your spot today. Do it quickly before all the spots are filled!

*Don't miss out on great food and a good time! You **MUST TEXT** me ASAP at (XXX) XXX-XXXX to **RSVP** your seat!*

*To stay up-to-date about future invasions, you can attend to get access to **AMAZING FOOD** at the best restaurants in town, **become a part of our community, and join (FACEBOOK GROUP NAME)**: Link*

See you soon!

Best Regards,

(your name)

P.S. *We would love to know about new, awesome foodie spots in town! Email us your favorite restaurant and we will try to set up our next invasion there!*

Be sure to connect with us on:

- *Facebook: Link*
- *Twitter: Link*
- *Instagram: Link*

Be sure to add the "P.S." because a lot of people will know an owner, or manager, of a restaurant and will refer you. This is great because they're doing the work for you. If I set up an event because of them, I'll tell that person to bring a few friends with them, and that their meal is on me as a thank you. This, of course, is because we want them to refer us to another business.

Social media

Remember to include your Facebook, Twitter, and Instagram links (plus any other social media you use) at the bottom of the flyer so you can keep in contact with everybody. I like to stick to the most popular social media programs right now. The majority use Facebook, Twitter, and Instagram.

Start a Facebook Foodie Group

As you saw in the flyer email, I mentioned a Facebook Group. Now, I haven't introduced this yet because this won't be relevant until you've built a substantial following on Facebook. But, once you do, you will need to start a Facebook Foodie Group.

This becomes incredibly convenient because you will invite all the individuals who usually come to your invasions. Then when you post about an upcoming event, they may ask to join, rather than you having to invite them. Also, sometimes people may not respond to emails or texts, so this creates another opportunity for them to get information about an upcoming event. You are also creating this exclusive club that people get to be apart of, and that adds a really nice touch to your invasions.

So, how do you make a Facebook Group? Follow these steps:

How do I create a group?

Computer Help   Mobile Help ▾   ➔ Share Article

To create a group:

1 Click ▾ in the top right of Facebook and select **Create Group**.

2 Enter your group name, add group members and then choose the privacy setting for your group.

3 Click **Create**.

Once you create your group, you personalize it by uploading a cover photo and adding a description.

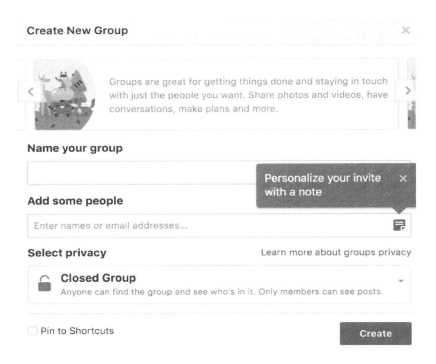

After coming up with a cool name, start inviting everyone possible, especially those that have joined you in other invasions or events because they already like the concept.

In case you are wondering why you are inviting people who haven't been to an invasion, it's because you're missing out an untapped market. Never assume people won't want to come to events, you just never know. Either way, inviting them isn't going to hurt.

Now that you have created your Facebook Foodie Group, start posting your upcoming invasions to keep the group involved and informed.

Increasing your email databases

Eventually, you'll be as busy as I am. As I've been doing this for a long time, I now have 10 email databases with 480 emails in just my first database. Google doesn't allow you to send more than 500 emails from one account a day, so I have multiple Gmail accounts. Again, if you don't use Gmail, you'll have to test the limit of your email service (Yahoo, Hotmail, etc.) yourself.

All in all, I email about 40,000 people every single week in Las Vegas. I realize that sounds like a lot—it sounds crazy to me too! When I first started doing this, I had high hopes, but I'd never imagined I could get 40,000 email addresses. If you do it for long enough though, it won't stop.

However, don't create multiple Gmail accounts until you need them—add the accounts as you grow. So let's say your database has grown and you need to send more emails—you'll need to start a new Gmail account.

Creating a new account

In my database folder, I've already emailed Database 1 with my original Gmail account. For Database 2, I had to start a new Gmail account. I'll double-click Database 2, go to Gmail again, and log into the new account. Select "New account" in Google and enter my new email address and password. When the new Gmail account comes up, I'll click "Compose", then "Bcc" to send my next 500 emails, enter the "Subject" as before, copy-and-paste the flyer text, and "Send".

111

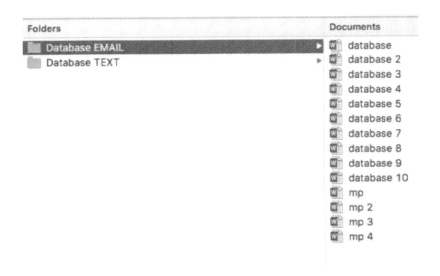

Paying for an email service

That's how I personally approach email databases, and it only takes me 10 minutes to send 500 emails every day. I'm not so busy that 10 minutes will harm my business or lose me money. Email, texting, and Facebook are free because you already pay for your cell phone—so it doesn't cost you anything and this method does work.

However, if you start getting 10,000 or more email addresses, you might want to pay for a service that does this easier and faster, such as MailChimp. You can Google search different services that send out unlimited emails (search for "email service to send unlimited emails in a single day from a database"). These services are sometimes referred to as "email blasters" and some offer free trials. For me, if I can keep it free, I'd rather keep it free.

Chapter 13

Wrapping It All Up

My intent with this book was to show you how much you can do, with what you already have, as effectively as you can, to make as much money as you can. Believe it or not, that's **all it takes**. In this chapter, I'll show you how to bring this concept together to make it work.

Getting restaurant owners on-board

Restaurant Invasions involve you approaching restaurants with a verbal presentation of how you can bring customers into their establishment during the slowest time, of their slowest day, to increase the restaurant's sales. For all of the customers you bring to the establishment during the agreed time, you'll receive 50% of the total sales.

During the presentation, you also inform the business owner that your Restaurant Invasion friends will use social media, such as Yelp, to check in and write reviews of their experience. This will give the business owners an opportunity to impress Yelp contributors by offering great customer service and amazing food. The perfect pitch includes being respectful and dressing professionally.

The SINALOA principle

However, even with the perfect pitch, your proposal may still be rejected. So, you need to be ready to give the restaurant owner the best reasons for accepting your proposal and show them how it will benefit their business.

To overcome rejections, you need to embrace the SINALOA principle—*Safety In Numbers And Law Of Averages*. The concept here is to ask as many businesses to participate in a Restaurant Invasion until one business agrees to it. Don't give up when you're rejected.

Cell phone contact list

Once an establishment has agreed to a Restaurant Invasion, it's time to start building your contact list and inviting all of your friends to the invasion. The first list to develop is your cell phone list. My recommendation is to text everyone two weeks before the Restaurant Invasion to chat with them generally, so when you invite them to the restaurant it won't sound so much like a pitch. This will also give you the opportunity to recognize a good contact from a bad contact.

Then, 48 hours later, text your friends to invite them to the Restaurant Invasion. During this conversation, you will find out some valuable information regarding your friends' schedule. With this information, you'll be able to create a spreadsheet of your friends' days off. This is a great tool to use so you know who to invite to specific restaurant invasions. Your cell phone contacts list is a valuable resource for your database.

Remember to follow the rules of contact:
- 2 weeks prior text to invite people
- 1 week prior to confirm
- 24 hours prior to remind them
- Follow-up text the next day to thank them

Facebook and other social media contacts

Facebook and other social media sites are great resources to build your database. When a phone number doesn't work, send a personal direct message to the person using Facebook. Do **not** write on their timeline or their wall. During the conversation, obtain their cell phone number. When you have their number, update their information in your cell phone contacts. The opportunity to build your database using Facebook (as well as Twitter, Instagram, etc.) is limitless.

Texting your contacts

The Notes application will help you manage your Restaurant Invasion invitations via text. It's also a great tool to use during an event to collect guests' information for your database. Once the information is collected, it is best to text all the guests within 24 hours to show your appreciation for their attendance at your event. If you text them within the 24-hour period, it is highly likely that they will remember you.

Another tool to use for texting is a mass texting app. This app allows you to make groups of people you can text. But, be careful you don't encounter "carrier throttling," which occurs when you text too many people, too fast, and your carrier cuts off your text messaging capabilities.

Follow-up email

When you finish texting everyone your appreciation, it's best to follow up with an email. Simply express your appreciation and say that you hope they had fun. If I have their phone numbers, I also follow up in a few days to see whether they received my email.

Using email, send everyone flyers regarding all future events. As your database grows, you will likely need to add more Gmail accounts to handle the volume of emails, as Google doesn't allow you to send more than 500 emails from one account per day.

Always hustle

Don't forget to always hustle. The true hustler will talk to a minimum of 10 new restaurants a day, every day, but you do what's comfortable for you. When you commit to a consistent schedule for yourself, you will establish better habits for your life. However, it's going to take a lot of work and confidence to achieve this. You can't become lazy when sending the emails or text messages.

It's really up to you how hard you're willing to hustle to reach your goal. You can get not only $250,000, but $500,000, or $750,000, or up to $1,000,000 a year if you really hustle.

Eat for free

As well as the earning potential, you'll eventually be able to go to any restaurant—even if it isn't an invasion—and eat anything you want. The owner won't charge you because you're helping them to make so much money, not only by leaving reviews on your Yelp account, but by using all the tools that are available and maximizing them.

Unlimited earning potential

I'm so excited for you because I know that if you do everything I've said, you'll start making some serious money. This income is all from eating for free, texting some people, putting an event together, and hanging out with your friends. That's all you have to do and from that, you can earn half a million dollars a year.

For those of you who are over-achievers, who are constantly taking the concept to the next level, you'll be able to earn much more than that! It's absolutely no joke when I say you could be making $250,000 to $1,000,000 a year from this concept.

If Mark Zuckerberg can become a 30-billion-dollar man, then why can't you make half a million dollars by using Facebook and other tools you already own? You can make that much money by finding people who are already on Facebook. All you have to do is invite these people to eat with you, or invite them to do things you're already doing.

Do something that you find entertainment in—by eating at restaurants or doing whatever you love. Maintain your relationships with people by letting them see the value of **you**. On the business side, the business owners will see nothing **but** your value.

You may end up like me, where all of your friends own businesses; where anything you need is at your disposal, because they're your friends now. You bring them business. You're putting money in their pockets, and feeding their kids with all of the revenue. People are going to fall in love with you.

Over to you...

Now, you have all of the information I had when I began this journey. Over the course of a few years, I grew this little idea into a six-figure yearly income. In total, I earned more than $1,000,000 in just a few years. There's nothing stopping you from earning a six-figure income by applying the techniques and strategies I've outlined in this book.

There is nothing "hard" here—you just need a willingness to step outside of your comfort zone and try something you've never tried before, exactly what you need to try anything new. If you had never tried windsurfing before, you'd have to go to a place you've never been (a windsurfing school), meet with people you've never spoken to (the instructors, receptionists, and other students taking the class), and do something you've never done before (stand on a windsurfing board and be prepared to fall in the water and look like an idiot until you figure it out).

The difference between my Restaurant Invasion strategy and starting windsurfing lessons is that one of these will results in you pocketing more money than you started with. One of these will turn your time into money. One of these will teach you new skills that will enable you to make a living. If it were me, I'd master the skills outlined in this book and, as the proverb says, learn to fish...

Now what?

Congratulations! You've finished the book. But, you are probably wondering what the next step is. The next step is simple: you're going to go back to the first page and reread this book!

That's right! Read it cover to cover for the second time. Then, a third time (on the bright side, it's short, so it shouldn't take you very long). Now, that might not be what you want to hear, but the reality is, it's going to take time for you to understand all of the techniques we went over. I'm sure you're eager to get out there and make a six-figure income from eating with your friends—but you need to master these practices.

Pitching might sound easy, but this is an art that will take time for you to conquer. Databasing might seem simple enough, but there are a lot of intricate parts to grasp before becoming successful at it.

Reread the book, take notes in the margins, highlight, and practice. That's the next step.

Do you want to know the best part? It's a step you'll never really complete. Yes, you'll eventually gain the confidence to pitch restaurants and host invasions. But, this book is a never-ending resource. You should always be referring back to it, rereading sections, even if you already achieved that six-figure income because it will only make you better.

I wish you all the best in your future, and I hope you take everything I've shared with you and apply it to give yourself the life you want and deserve.

Have questions? Let's talk

Now, technically, there is another step you can take before rereading the book. To prove that I want you to truly succeed, I'm going to give you my personal contact information in case you have questions or need advice.

Just text **702-348-5618**: "I just finished reading How to Eat Your Way to a 6-Figure Income."

Within 24 hours, I will reach out, congratulate you on completing this book, and answer any questions you may have.

You **can** do this, and I'm gonna do my very best to support you in your journey!

Hope to hear from you soon!

Made in the USA
Middletown, DE
05 October 2022

12051605R00068